A Media Research Institute Survey

America's Leading Daily Newspapers

Michael Emery, Director
Media Research Institute

R.J. Berg & Company, Publishers
Indianapolis, Indiana 46220
1983

America's
Leading
Daily
Newspapers

Preface

This is the first in a series of continuing studies conducted by the Media Research Institute, founded in 1982 within the Department of Journalism at California State University, Northridge. The purpose of MRI is to sponsor studies of media performance, particulary news media, and to determine attitudes about that performance.

It is hoped that these studies, beginning with *America's Leading Daily Newspapers,* will appeal to media professionals, journalism professors, high school and college journalism students, and in some instances the general public.

While a number of academic publications deal in part with media performance, many of these studies are heavily quantitative and narrow in focus. Several other publications and journalism reviews carry essays and articles dealing with current media problems. MRI's goal is to develop broad-based qualitative and quantitative studies and descriptions that supplement these other research efforts.

While the primary purpose of MRI is to examine the performance of news media, it is expected that studies dealing with various aspects of other media will be considered.

Michael Emery, Director
Media Research Institute

viii

Contents

INTRODUCTION

This newspaper study was designed to judge perception of general quality. It was recognized that few of the more than three thousand publishers, editors, and journalism professors polled would be intimately familiar with all of the leading daily newspapers. However, it was assumed that nearly all of them could immediately name their favorite newspapers, based on their reading of professional journals and trade magazines, professional associations, past knowledge, and instincts. Thus, this study shows which papers are thought to be the best.

Questionnaires were sent to every daily newspaper and to every nationally affiliated journalism professor at both four-year and two-year colleges and universities. The Media Research Institute received 610 responses. There was strong evidence that the survey was taken seriously. There were a number of spontaneous comments about the quality of certain papers, some of them quite enthusiastic.

Each person was asked to indicate his or her choice of papers that belonged on a "top 10" list, following the tradition of other studies dating to 1960. These selections were not ranked. However, unlike previous studies done by public opinion expert Edward L. Bernays, *Time* magazine, and *Adweek*, this survey asked a number of other questions. Respondents were asked to rank their choices for a "top 5" list. They also were asked to rank their choices for a "top 5" in their particular region of the nation, as determined by a map used by *Editor & Publisher*.

They also were asked to name other favorites: cartoonist, the best-designed newspaper, press association, editorial page, and sports section. However, this information could not be tabulated because of the wide variety of responses and the proclivity of people to name their hometown paper. But, it should be noted, this kind of provincialism or boosterism was not noticeable in the selection of national and regional leaders. There was less evidence of regional bias than expected, where respondents might have put local favorites ahead of more logical choices in the "top 10" or "top 5" rankings. This lack of bias was especially noticeable in the rankings for the "top 5."

In addition, there was a representative sampling of responses from the various sections of the nation. For example, 26% of the responses came from eight heavily populated Midwestern states—Minnesota through Ohio—where many long-standing daily newspapers and journalism departments are evidence of tradition that runs deep. The New England, New York-New Jersey-Pennsylvania, and Mid-Atlantic regions produced 28%; the Far West, Rocky Mountain and Southwestern regions added 25%; and the Deep South and Texas-Oklahoma-Louisiana regions totaled 21%.

There also was a remarkably even distribution in responses from professionals and educators. Of the 610 responses, 292 came from newspapers (48%) and 318 from journalism educators (52%). Approximately 24% of 1,300 educators polled responded, along with 17% of 1,-730 editors and publishers.

Of those 1,730 dailies polled, 85% were in the under-50,000 circulation class. The survey showed that 234 of the 292 newspaper responses, or 80%, came from that size paper. In the 50,000 to 100,000 class (8% nationally), the survey produced an 8% rate. From 100,000 to 250,000 (5% nationally), the poll showed 6%. The next range, 250,000 to 500,000 (2% nationally), responded at 3%. And of the largest papers, more than 500,000 (roughly 1% nationally), the survey showed a return from seven of the fourteen papers, or 2% of all papers responding. (These figures were rounded to the nearest percentage point.)

It is clear that while national surveys cannot rank newspapers with absolute precision, the respondents eliminated some newspapers with large circulations and doubtful quality. Newspapers that have been consistent in fulfilling their obligations to offer comprehensive coverage and to express themselves courageously on the editorial page deserve this kind of professional recognition.

There are flaws, of course. The maintenance of a sound publishing tradition sometimes gives a paper a chance to live on that reputation after the quality has diminished. This may be true in some cases with papers described in this monograph. However, the survey also determined growing enthusiasm for certain papers that were ranked lower in previous studies. The brilliance of certain writers or departments (such as a Washington bureau) was not measured here. Hopefully, these achievements are rewarded elsewhere, through various prizes. It is possible that certain papers do a better over-all job than their professional and academic judges realize. Nonetheless, the perception of quality is what makes a reputation.

The descriptive material that supplements the "Summary of the Survey" offers both historical and current information about the leading newspapers, in addition to mentioning many other papers in the various regions. This supportive information is partially derived from *The Press and America* by Edwin and Michael Emery. The fifth edition of this journalism history, published by Prentice-Hall, Inc., will appear in early 1984, marking its 30th anniversary. It will contain a summary of these and past survey results in a chapter on today's leading newspapers. A summary of the study appeared in the 11 June 1983 *Editor & Publisher.*

AMERICA'S LEADING DAILY NEWSPAPERS

Summary of the Survey

The top five papers, in order, were the *New York Times, Wall Street Journal, Washington Post, Los Angeles Times,* and *Chicago Tribune.*

The *Christian Science Monitor* was in sixth place and closely bunched in the next group—in no particular order—were the *Philadelphia Inquirer, Boston Globe,* and *Miami Herald.*

Right behind, also in no particular ranking, were the *Louisville Courier-Journal, St. Petersburg Times, Newsday, Atlanta Constitution, Milwaukee Journal,* and *St. Louis Post-Dispatch.*

There was no attempt to produce specific rankings for positions after sixth place because the results were extremely close, some evidence of bias appeared, and the numbers would not have been meaningful. But those in the top six spots were clear-cut favorites for their specific position, and those in the next three positions outdistanced the remaining half dozen when national "top 10" votes, mentions in the "top 5" rankings, and the regional rankings were compared for consistency.

Gains in prestige were attributed to the *Chicago Tribune, Philadelphia Inquirer, Boston Globe, St. Petersburg Times,* and *Newsday. USA Today* was not included in this study because it was not in full operation at the time.

Unlike previous studies, this one attempted to differentiate between regional strength and national reputation. Evaluation of the "top 5" and "top 10" rankings, nationally and by region, led to the ranking of the six papers with clear national strength in nearly every region and the isolation of another nine with a mixture of regional and national recognition. A number of other newspapers, all mentioned in this monograph, received regional support but little if any national attention. A one-to-five scoring method was used to determine rankings within regions and the "top 5." There was a consistency with the "top 10" results, as the tables show.

The *New York Times,* the leader in all polls since the first one in 1960, was listed as being in the top ten by 95% of the respondents and in the top five by 89%. Next was the *Wall Street Journal,* the nation's circulation leader, with figures of 90% and 76%.

The *Washington Post* nipped the *Los Angeles Times* for third place, gaining figures of 87.5% and 75% to the Western giant's 84.5% and 68.5%. The *Chicago Tribune* was a clear fifth, with 79% and 36.5%.

When looking further at the "top 5" rankings, the *New York Times* was listed as the top newspaper by 368 of the 610 respondents, or 60%. The *Wall Street Journal* received 111 first places (18%); *Washington Post,* 35; *Los Angeles Times,* 15; and *Chicago Tribune,* 6.

The *Washington Post* got the most second place marks, 192, to 108 for the *New York Times,* 100 for *Wall Street Journal,* and 68 for *Los Angeles Times.* The *Washington Post* and *Los Angeles Times* were locked in a battle for third place listings, with Washington leading 136 to 132. The *Wall Street Journal* had 112.

Separate rankings by regions showed the *St. Petersburg Times* edging the *Atlanta Constitution* for the number two position in the South and receiving by far the most mentions as the paper with the nation's best graphic design. *Newsday* and the *Baltimore Sun* remained popular in their area, along with the *Dallas Morning News* and to a lesser extent the *Dallas Times Herald* in the Southwest, *Seattle Times* and *San Francisco Chronicle* in the West, and *Kansas City Times, Chicago Sun-Times, Minneapolis Star and Tribune, Detroit Free Press,* and *Des Moines Register* in the nation's center.

Regional Comparison
of Top Ten Rankings

Region	1	2	3	4	5	6	7	8	9
NYT	1-2	1	1	1	1	1	1-2	1-2	3-4
WSJ	1-2	3	2	3	2	2	1-2	3	2
WP	4	2	3	2	5	3	3-4	1-2	3-4
LAT	5	4	4	4	3-4	4	3-4	4	1
CT	7	9	6-7	6	3-4	5	5	5	5
CSM	6	8	9	8	7	6	6-7	8	6

NOTE: The *Boston Globe* was 3 in region one; 5 in region two; 6 in region four, six, and nine. The *Miami Herald* was 5 in regions three and four and 6 in regions two and five. The *Philadelphia Inquirer* was 7 in region two and 8 in region seven. The *Atlanta Constitution* was 7 in region eight and 8 in region one. The *Louisville Courier-Journal* was 6 to 7 in region three. The rest of the results were scattered; there was a sharp drop in numbers in most regions after the first four places, with only one or two votes separating newspapers in several cases. The voting for the top four also was often close, but a fairly consistent pattern developed.

Regional Comparison
of Top Five Rankings

Region	1	2	3	4	5	6	7	8	9
NYT	1	1	1	1	1	1	1	1	1
WSJ	3	3	2	2	2	3	2	3	4
WP	2	2	3	3	3	2	3	2	2
LAT	4	4	4	4	4	4	4	4	3
CT	8	6	-*	6	5	6	6	6	6
CSM	5	-*	7	8	6	5	7	5	5

*This indicates the newspaper finished too low to allow a ranking.

NOTE: Again there was a pattern in the first four positions, with the *Washington Post* gaining on the *Wall Street Journal* in a reversal of the "top 10" rankings. There was a sharp drop off starting with the fifth position, where this time the *Chicago Tribune* faced stiff competition from the *Christian Science Monitor* and the *Philadelphia Inquirer*. The *Miami Herald* and *Boston Globe* slipped a few notches here. The *Philadelphia Inquirer* was 5 in regions two and seven and 5 to 6 in region three with the *Louisville Courier-Journal*. The *Miami Herald* was 5 in region four. The *Boston Globe* was 7 in regions two, six, eight, and nine. The *St. Petersburg Times* was 7 in region four and 8 in region three. The rest of the results were inconclusive except for showing evidence of scattered national recognition; these mentions solidified some positions in the "top 15" as did similar mentions in the "top 10" rankings. These papers required strong regional strength to be weighed with their smaller national totals.

Regional Voting Patterns

Region	Educators	Editors/Publishers	Under 50,000	50,000-100,000	100,000-250,000	250,000-500,000	More Than 500,000
1	14	13	11	1	1		3
2	54	37	22	5	6	1	
3	31	22	17	4	1		
4	29	29	24	4	1		
5	86	73	59	4	4	3	3
6	29	37	34		1	2	
7	14	23	21	1	1		
8	11	16	12	2		2	
9	50	42	34	3	3	1	1
TOTALS	**318**	**219**	**234**	**24**	**18**	**9**	**7**

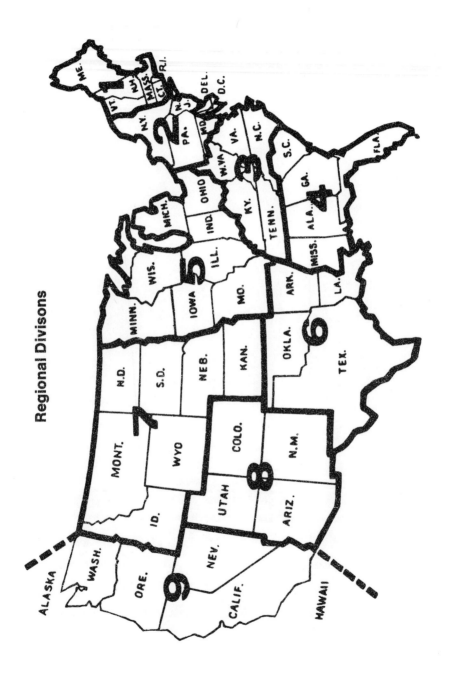

The New York Times

The *New York Times* was judged the best overall newspaper in all nine regions. From the Deep South to the Pacific Northwest, survey respondents gave their highest acclaim to the *Times,* as other respondents did in the previous polls dating to 1960. For the past seventy-five years the *Times,* "the paper of record" since those days of Adolph S. Ochs and Carr Van Anda, has enjoyed enormous international prestige.

From the day of its founding, 18 September 1851, the *Times* has for the most part eschewed the sensationalism employed by other New York dailies. Henry J. Raymond and George Jones were partners in the beginning, with Raymond seeking to have their paper excel in reporting foreign events. As the years passed the *Times* built a strong reputation, helping to destroy the Tweed Ring in 1871 by exposing the amazing story of corruption. Yet the paper began to experience financial problems and had to be rescued from financial ruin by Ochs in 1896.

During the next twenty-five years Ochs, assisted by the genius of his legendary managing editor Van Anda, developed a formula for success. The paper took in $100 million during that quarter century, and all but 4 percent was used to improve the product. By the time of World War I the paper had recorded a series of scoops on historic events, including the climactic battle of the Russo-Japanese War and the sinking of the Titanic.

The paper also had become a prime source of information for readers eager to obtain the full text of a presidential speech, congressional debate, or foreign treaty. On any big news day the *Times* could be counted on to fill its pages with date lined stories from around the world as its foreign staff grew in size.

Politically the paper was Democratic, except during the campaigns of Williams Jennings Bryan, but was essentially conservative in tone. Ochs was not a "crusader" in the public interest, as were William Randolph Hearst and Joseph Pulitzer. But his paper did support the League of Nations plan of President Woodrow Wilson, and stuck with the Democrats until 1940, when the paper switched to Republican Wendall Willkie.

A number of management crises occurred in the late 1960s which eventually resulted in Abe Rosenthal becoming executive editor. Publication of the Pentagon Papers in 1971 brought the paper further glory, in a continuation of the "paper of record" tradition. However, changing condi-

"All the News That's Fit to Print"

The New York Times

Weather: New York, partly sunny and warm. Midwest, fair. South, scattered showers and thunderstorms. West and Southwest, mostly fair, some widely scattered showers and thunderstorms. Details on page 44.

VOL.CXXXII . . . . No. 45,719 — Copyright © 1983 The New York Times — NEW YORK, FRIDAY, JUNE 24, 1983 — Y — 50 CENTS

SUPREME COURT, 7-2, RESTRICTS CONGRESS'S RIGHT TO OVERRULE ACTIONS BY EXECUTIVE BRANCH

U.S. CALLS POLICIES OF SOUTH AFRICANS 'MORALLY WRONG'

REAGAN STANCE OUTLINED

Official Terms End of Apartheid Certain and Says Aiding in Peaceful Shift Is Vital

By BERNARD GWERTZMAN

Special to The New York Times

WASHINGTON, June 23 — The Reagan Administration said today that South Africa's policy of racial separation would inevitably be scrapped and that it was crucial for the United States to help make sure the change was peaceful rather than violent.

In the Administration's most comprehensive statement on southern Africa in nearly two years, Lawrence S. Eagle-

Excerpts from speech, page 6.

burger, Under Secretary of State for Political Affairs, said the United States viewed South Africa's political system as "morally wrong."

"We stand against injustice, and therefore we must reject the legal and political premises and consequences of apartheid," Mr. Eagleburger said in a speech prepared for delivery tonight in San Francisco to the National Conference of Editorial Writers.

Rebutting 'Misconceptions'

A senior official in Washington said that the Administration's policies on southern Africa had been worked out and that it was considered important and timely to make the policies public to rebut continuing "misconceptions," particularly that the Administration does not oppose apartheid strongly enough.

Mr. Eagleburger also indicated that the Administration, hoping to conclude the long effort to create independence for South-West Africa, had worked out new language to try to persuade Angola to agree to the withdrawal of Cuban combat troops from its territory in return for a South African pullout from the southern areas of Angola and the granting of independence to South-West Africa as the nation of Namibia.

Linkage Dropped for 'Reciprocity'

Soon after President Reagan took office, the Administration said Cuban withdrawal from Angola and South African withdrawal from Namibia had to be linked. But as a result of criticism of that approach from some allies as well as Angola's refusal to agree to link the two steps directly, the Administration said today that it was not seeking linkage but "reciprocity."

"South Africa must leave Angola's southern provinces and it must leave Namibia," Mr. Eagleburger said. "Angola, on the other hand, can make such steps possible, while remaining true to its principles, by assuring, as a separate sovereign act, the withdrawal of Cuban combat forces from its territory."

Reagan Ready to Use Influence

He said Mr. Reagan was prepared "to use his full influence" to bring about Namibia's independence and "a peaceful and independent Angola in a peaceful and prosperous region."

On South Africa, Mr. Eagleburger said that the apartheid system would be changed in South Africa but that the key question was how this would be brought about — peacefully or through revolution.

"By one means or another," he said,

Continued on Page 6, Column 1

INSIDE

Challenger Flight Hailed

As the crew prepared to return home, officials of the space agency said the six-day voyage of the shuttle was "nearly a perfect mission." Page 8.

U.S. Catholic Study Ordered

Pope John Paul II named three American prelates to find out why membership in religious orders in the United States has dropped. Page 9.

Buyer for Stravinsky Papers

A private Swiss foundation has agreed to pay $5.25 million for the archive of manuscripts and letters of the composer Igor Stravinsky. Page 23.

Around New York	16	Movies	20-21
Around the Nation	8	Music	17-18,23
Around the World	5	Obituaries	28
Art	22	Op-Ed	27
Books	23	Real Estate	14
Bridge	23	Restaurants	21
Business Day	29-41,44	Sports	24-25
Crossword	23	Style	15
Dance	19,22-23	Theaters	19-20
Day by Day	16	Washington Talk	10
Editorials	26	Weather	44
Letters	26	Weekend	17-23

News Summary and Index, Page 2

Classified Ads and Auto Exchange, Pages 42-43

United Press International

POPE RETURNS HOME: John Paul II met with Lech Walesa before ending Polish trip. Page 4.

New York Board Acts to Increase Rent Guidelines

By LEE A. DANIELS

New York City's Rent Guidelines Board, in a raucous five-hour meeting that was twice stopped by shouting and sign-waving demonstrators, yesterday approved basic increases of 4, 7 and 10 percent for the 300,000 rent-stabilized apartments whose leases expire in the year beginning Oct. 1.

The percentage increases, which apply to one-, two- and three-year leases, respectively, are the same guidelines that the board approved in 1982.

The board also acted to compensate more accurately the owners of apartments renting for $200 a month or less, and it approved a complex provision allowing a special one-time surcharge — a vacancy allowance — of up to 15 percent on apartments that had been vacant before being rented.

Under the provision, whether the surcharge can be levied and how much it can be are dependent on when the apartment was last vacant.

The board's actions, in the Police Department auditorium at 1 Police Plaza in lower Manhattan, were condemned by spokesmen for both landlords, who dominated the overflow audience, and tenants. The landlords said the increases were too small, and the tenants said they were too large.

The meeting followed the traditional

Continued on Page 44, Column 1

CONGRESS ADOPTS 1984 BUDGET PLAN

Both Houses Spurn Reagan in Approving a Bill to Spend $849 Billion Next Year

By STEVEN V. ROBERTS

Special to The New York Times

WASHINGTON, June 23 — Over the strenuous objections of President Reagan, both houses of Congress approved a compromise 1984 Federal budget today that mandates higher taxes, lower military spending and more domestic spending than the Administration requested.

The House vote, which came first, was 239 to 186. Early this evening the Senate followed suit, 51 to 43.

The spending plan, which apportions $849.6 billion for the fiscal year beginning Oct. 1, took almost two weeks to produce in a House-Senate conference. The deficit is projected to range from $170 billion to $179 billion, depending on how much Congress decides to spend for recession relief measures.

A Coalition of Moderates

To many lawmakers, the Congressional action signifies the emergence of a bipartisan coalition of moderates from both parties who differ significantly with the President's economic priorities.

"This indicates," said Representative Richard A. Gephardt, Democrat of Missouri, "that what has been called

The House voted, 229 to 191, to limit the benefits of the July 1 cut in income tax rates to $720 per filer. Page 11.

the 'grand coalition' is in the driver's seat on basic economic policy."

Ten Republicans joined 229 Democrats in approving the budget in the House, while 33 Democrats and 153 Republicans voted against it. In the Senate, the Republican leadership largely backed the budget in defiance of Mr. Reagan.

Howard H. Baker Jr. of Tennessee, the Senate majority leader, agonized all week about whether to support the President or his own committee chairman, Senator Pete V. Domenici, the New Mexico Republican who helped forge the compromise. Senator Baker,

Continued on Page 11, Column 1

Warren E. Burger: *"We have not yet found a better way to preserve freedom than by making the exercise of power subject to the carefully crafted restraints spelled out in the Constitution."*

Associated Press

Byron R. White: *"The increasing reliance of Congress upon the legislative veto suggests that the alternatives to which Congress must now turn are not entirely satisfactory."*

The New York Times/D. Gorton

Charles E. Grassley: *"It probably means that there's going to be very narrow writing of legislation in the future."*

Elliott H. Levitas: *"It's going to cripple the things that this President, or any President, will be able to do."*

Impact of the Decision

Political and Legal Experts Predict Changes In Relationship Between the Two Branches

By STEVEN R. WEISMAN

Special to The New York Times

News Analysis

WASHINGTON, June 23 — In its decision today the Supreme Court dramatically altered the relationship between Congress and the executive branch and created myriad new difficulties in their struggles to accommodate each other.

Legal and political experts predicted that the decision would lead to renewed jockeying over prerogatives and a search for new mechanisms allowing Congress to oversee executive decisions even as it grants the President power to spend money, wage war or take other actions.

The courts, in turn, are likely to be asked immediately whether certain executive powers are still valid. These powers were often declared by Presidents to be inherent in the office in the absence of legislation from Congress. In response, Congress would specifically grant the authority, reserving the right to block certain Presidential actions.

For example, does the President have the right to refuse to spend funds appropriated by Congress, now that the High Court has removed Congress's right to overturn such a move? May a President keep American troops committed to hostilities or sell arms overseas now that Congress may no longer veto such actions?

It is virtually certain that these and other questions affecting 200 statutes with legislative vetoes will be determined ultimately by Congress and the President themselves. As they address the matter, two competing historical forces will be at work.

First is the trend of the last 50 years of Presidents seeking from the Congress greater and greater power to regulate industry and commerce, to act swiftly in foreign policy, and to reorganize and run an increasingly complex Federal Government.

The second trend is the one mounted by both liberals and conservatives in the past 15 years aimed at curbing the President's power.

Limits on Powers Sought

Liberals, alarmed by Vietnam and Watergate, have led the fight to limit a President's ability to commit troops overseas, aid certain countries militarily and freeze funds already appropriated by Congress, as President Nixon did in the impoundment controversy of a decade ago.

More recently, conservatives have sought to limit the ability of the Federal Trade Commission, the Food and Drug Administration and other semi-independent Federal agencies to impose certain regulations on business.

Indeed, there was a certain irony in today's court decision for President Reagan. In the 1980 election campaign, Mr. Reagan favored the concept of legislative veto to curb the power of Federal agencies. As Presi-

Continued on Page 13, Column 3

POWERS MAY SHIFT

Justices Sweep Aside the 50-Year-Old Practice Affecting 200 Laws

By LINDA GREENHOUSE

Special to The New York Times

WASHINGTON, June 23 — The Supreme Court today swept aside a 50-year-old practice used by Congress to delegate authority to the President and then block his action under the law when it disagreed.

The Court, by a historic 7-to-2 vote, struck down this so-called legislative veto, saying that it violated constitutional requirements preserving the separation of powers.

Legislative veto provisions, which spell out and often restrict the Presi-

Excerpts are on page 12.

dent's authority under the law, have been written into about 200 statutes.

The ruling may profoundly alter the balance of power between the White House and Congress. It presumably strips Congress, for example, of the unilateral power it gained under the War Powers Resolution of 1973 to require the President to withdraw American troops from foreign hostilities.

From Hoover Presidency

The legislative veto procedure dates to 1932, when Congress added it to an appropriations bill to give President Hoover authority to reorganize the Government.

Under a legislative veto, either or both houses by a simple majority can block specific actions that the President or a Federal agency takes to carry out authority that Congress has delegated.

As a result of today's ruling, Congress will be able to disapprove executive branch action only if a bill to that effect passes both houses and receives the President's signature. If the President vetoes the legislation, Congress may block the President's action only by overriding his veto by a two-thirds vote.

The initial Congressional reaction was that the ruling would create "conflict and chaos" on Capitol Hill. There were differing views today as to whether it would give the President or Congress the upper hand over the long run.

Immigration Case Before Court

Some said the decision would give Presidents more power in certain key areas. Others others argued that the ruling would make Congress more reluctant than ever to grant certain powers to the President in the first place.

The decision, written by Chief Justice Warren E. Burger, came in a relatively minor immigration case, one of several legislative veto cases before the Court. The Justices had wrestled with the case for nearly two years, hearing argument in February 1982 and again last October.

The legislative veto has been a subject of debate for years among politicians, political scientists and legal scholars, many of whom awaited the

Continued on Page 13, Column 4

Sharp Shifts in Congress Practices And Legislative Conflict Predicted

Special to The New York Times

WASHINGTON, June 23 — Congressional supporters and opponents of the legislative veto agreed today that the Supreme Court decision would create conflict on Capitol Hill and significantly alter the way Congress conducts its business.

They predicted that in place of the legislative veto, which was struck down today by the Supreme Court, Congress would pass tighter restrictions on Presidential authority and rely more heavily on the power of the purse and overseeing authority.

"This decision is going to create a lot of conflict and chaos," said Senator Carl Levin, Democrat of Michigan.

"We're either going to tie the President's hands too much, and require the President to come to Congress for everything, or we're going to give him too much power," the Senator said. "We're going to be losing the subtlety of a flexible mechanism."

Several chairmen of Congressional committees said they would hold hearings to evaluate the Supreme Court decision. The decision is also expected to spawn Congressional proposals to let Congress to retain some formal veto authority within the restrictions of the decision.

Some liberal House members said they would introduce legislation that would require a joint resolution of approval of arms sales above a certain amount now that Congress has lost its right to disapprove such sales through a legislative veto. Such a resolution would be subject to a Presidential veto.

Similarly, some conservative House members have called for new legislation to deal with what they consider "regulatory abuses," now that Congress can no longer veto regulations.

Representative Elliot H. Levitas, Democrat of Georgia, the chief Congressional champion of the legislative

Continued on Page 13, Column 2

United Press International

ARAFAT ACCUSES SYRIA: Yasir Arafat, leader of the Palestine Liberation Organization, with guards yesterday near Tripoli, Lebanon. He said Syria was behind rebellion against him by Al Fatah dissidents. Page 6.

Accord on Medicaid Costs Reached in Albany

By MICHAEL ORESKES

Special to The New York Times

ALBANY, June 23 — Governor Cuomo and the legislative leaders agreed today on a plan to help New York City and the 57 counties outside the city deal with the rapidly rising costs of Medicaid.

The announcement was hailed by Mayor Koch and other officials. They termed the compromise a major breakthrough in an eight-year battle in which the city and the state's counties had argued that rising Medicaid costs threatened their fiscal solvency and forced them to increase local taxes.

Under the program, which would be phased in over three years, the local share of costs for long-term care, such as nursing homes and home health care, would be reduced from 25 to 10 percent.

New York City would save about $263 million next year, or about $12 million more than it is saving this year under a temporary Medicaid assistance program. In 1986, when the program would take full effect, the city would save an estimated $445 million, or $205 more than it is saving now. The amount would continue to rise with Medicaid costs.

The agreement was announced as the

Continued on Page 44, Column 1

tions in New York later brought problems to the *Times*. Faced with a deterioration of its advertising revenues and readership appeal, the *Times* brightened its typographical appearance, took aim at younger readers with "Weekend" and "Living" sections like other major dailies, and generally streamlined its operation under Rosenthal's able guidance. The revised editorial leadership continued with little change into the 1980s. Associate editors were Tom Wicker and Charlotte Curtis, who edited the "op-ed" page. Seymour Topping was managing editor, and Arthur Gelb, metropolitan editor. Hedrick Smith, winner of a Pulitzer Prize covering Moscow, headed the Washington bureau while Robert B. Semple, Jr. replaced James L. Greenfield as foreign editor. In 1980 the *Times* launched a national edition, printed by satellite transmission in Chicago, Florida, and California. By 1983 it was circulating one hundred thousand daily and two hundred thousand Sunday, 20 percent home-delivered.

In general the *Times* has been staunchly internationalistic in its world outlook and somewhat in the middle on domestic events, leaning to the progressive side in the past thirty years. The paper supported Roosevelt in 1944, jumped to Republicans Dewey and Eisenhower in 1948, 1952, and 1956, and then headed back into the Democratic column for six consecutive elections. By 1983 the *Times* had won a record fifty-three Pulitzer Prizes. Its circulation was 963,000 on weekdays.

The Wall Street Journal

The widespread recognition given the *Wall Street Journal* apparently ended any controversy over whether the paper belonged in such a survey of the so-called "regular" newspapers. The nation's largest circulation newspaper in 1983 with 2,036,000 copies each morning, the *Wall Street Journal* received strong support from every region. Adding to its reputation, no doubt, was its satellite transmission service to seventeen printing plants.

Bernard Kilgore gave the paper its current style when in 1940 he assumed the managing editor's position and broadened its solid financial coverage to include lucidly written summaries of vital national and world events and comprehensive stories that interpreted trends in industry. The paper had been founded in 1889 by Charles H. Dow as the voice of the Dow Jones and Company financial news service.

By 1960 the *Journal's* circulation had jumped past seven hundred thousand, following the expansion to eight printing plants across the nation. By 1976 the figure had jumped to 1,450,000, second only to the *New York Daily News,* with those positions destined to be reversed. Before Kilgore's death in 1967, he had seen his editors and staff writers win a number of

THE WALL STREET JOURNAL.

© 1983 Dow Jones & Company, Inc. All Rights Reserved.

VOL. CVIII NO. 122   ★ ★ ★   WESTERN EDITION   THURSDAY, JUNE 23, 1983   RIVERSIDE, CALIF.   40 CENTS

Troubled Waters

Sweden Says It Believes That Soviet Sub Visits Reflect War Planning

Theory Holds That U.S.S.R. Is Studying the Coastline, Testing Swedes' Defenses

Prowling Stockholm Harbor

By WALTER S. MOSSBERG
Staff Reporter of THE WALL STREET JOURNAL

WASHINGTON—In October 1981, when Defense Secretary Caspar Weinberger visited Sweden, the Swedish navy took him to visit the largest, most secret and most impressive facility, the Musko Naval Base.

The base, which guards the rocky archipelago between Stockholm and the Baltic Sea, is startling to see. It is carved into the side of a coastal mountain, admitting submarines and surface ships to underground piers through a huge camouflaged portal that can be closed with blast-protection doors.

Exactly a year later, Swedish officials now believe, Soviet military representatives also visited Musko's waters—secretly. They came in a fleet of six submarines, including bottom-crawling "midget subs" that prowled the nearby sea floor amid secret electronic detectors and communication devices Sweden has planted there.

In recent weeks, Sweden has communicated to the U.S. an ominous theory to explain why Moscow has sent subs across the Baltic to Musko and to some of its other politically and militarily sensitive coastal areas since 1982.

Updating Plans for War

Swedish officials have concluded that the submarine incursions are part of a crash effort by the Soviet Union to update its battle plans for conventional war in Europe. The Swedes aren't predicting that war is imminent, but they do believe the Soviets are testing Swedish defenses—and studying key coastal sites—in order to develop detailed war plans.

U.S. defense officials confirm that they have received this assessment and that the Pentagon is studying carefully the Swedish evidence of an urgent effort by Moscow to update its war plans.

However, American officials haven't decided yet whether they agree with the Swedish theory, and they won't say much about it. In part, this is because Sweden might be embarrassed if it appeared that U.S. and Swedish experts were working together on the problem of Soviet intentions. Sweden isn't a member of the North Atlantic Treaty Organization and has a policy of neutrality.

Nevertheless, oil indications are that the cooperation is extensive, though the contacts are kept under cover both in Stockholm and at the Pentagon. Carl Bildt, a conservative member of the Swedish Parliament who served on the official commission investigating the Musko incident, caused an uproar at home in May when he visited Washington and met with officials at the Pentagon and elsewhere, presumably to discuss the submarine threat.

A U.S. naval official, after refusing to disclose the nature of U.S.-Swedish contacts on the matter, says: "You can figure out for yourself that we wouldn't exactly want to be bystanders on a thing like this." One reason for the U.S. interest is that, despite Sweden's neutrality, it is a well-

armed nation that NATO war plans assume would count any Soviet military moves. NATO strategists fear that in wartime he can sweep and planes from the Baltic coast and the Skovskansk area might try to swarm across Sweden into neighboring Norway. The location and lengthy Norwegian coastline truths that NATO makes two its controlling the flow of Soviet submarines into the North Atlantic from Arctic waters.

According to the Swedish commission's report, released in April, there have been more than 40 incursions by Soviet submarines in 1982 and 1983 into Sweden territorial waters, many of them near major cities, strategic inlets and sensitive naval bases. Last September, it is believed, Soviet subs prowled Stockholm Harbor during a visit by then U.S. warships.

The Soviet patrols reported in Norwegian waters have taken place even deep within the fjords that penetrate Norway's coast. And in light of the Swedish findings, other

Please Turn to Page 16, Column 1

What's News—

Business and Finance

CONSUMER PRICES rose in May an adjusted 0.5%, or at a 6% annual rate before compounding, mainly because of higher fuel prices. The Labor Department also said gross weekly pay of U.S. workers rose an adjusted 0.6% in May.

(Story on Page 2)

Metromedia agreed to buy original programs made by Time Inc.'s Home Box Office pay-cable TV unit.

(Story on Page 4)

Viacom agreed with Vistavision Cable, a U.K. concern, to develop cable TV in Britain. The accord is the latest in a series of alliances by U.S. communications companies entering fledgling overseas pay-TV markets.

(Story on Page 4)

The SEC could be turned further right by Reagan in the next year as he fills the commission's three expected vacancies. The positions currently are held by three moderate commissioners, Barbara Thomas, John Evans and Bevis Longstreth.

(Story on Page 3)

Exxon and Columbia Gas Transmission, charging that Columbia is buying less gas and paying lower prices than stipulated in contracts.

(Story on Page 10)

Imasco will receive an $172-a-share offer for Canadian Tire for $75 a share, or $1.11 billion (Canadian). Imasco hinted the offer mightn't receive widespread bidder support, and some company observers suggested the bid might be sweetened further.

(Story on Page 4)

CSX's proposed acquisition of Texas Gas may help it become the first transportation company to offer one-stop shipping. The Justice Department indicated it doesn't intend to oppose bids for Texas Gas by CSX or Coastal Corp., which had pledged to further sweeten its takeover offer.

(Story on Page 3)

John De Lorean plans to ask investors for money to bring his company out of bankruptcy proceedings and to resume production of its stainless-steel sports car. But creditors' lawyers call the plan a ruse to delay the company's liquidation.

(Story on Page 3)

IBM is cutting prices as much as 30% on main processors used with its 4300 system and is introducing a small processor that is more powerful than its existing model.

(Story on Page 3)

The U.S. dollar continued to fall against most major European currencies despite higher American interest rates. Gold rose $1.50 an ounce to $420.30 on the Comex.

(Story on Page 6)

Allegheny International is selling its 37.3% stake in Liquid Air to the parent, L'Air Liquide S.A. of France, for $116.5 million.

(Story on Page 4)

California Canners, the second-largest fruit and vegetable canning cooperative in the U.S., plans to lease much of its operation to Tri-Valley Growers, the largest cooperative, in a move it said was the only alternative to selling its assets.

(Story on Page 6)

Trafalgar House's bid for Peninsular & Oriental Steam Navigation was blocked for as long as six months when the British government asked its antitrust agency to review the offer.

(Story on Page 10)

Portugal's new coalition government, which has proposed an economic austerity program, devalued the escudo 12%.

(Story on Page 34)

United Technologies received a $56 million Air Force contract for aircraft-engine parts.

(Story on Page 35)

Markets—

Stocks: Volume 110,220,000 shares. Dow Jones industrials 1240.48, off 1.71; transportation 561.65, off 1.58; utilities 128.74, up 0.45.

Bonds: Dow Jones 20 bonds 73.60, up 0.44.

Commodities: Dow Jones futures index 146.95, up 0.65; spot index 143.42, up 1.24.

World-Wide

POPE JOHN PAUL II MET Polish leader Jaruzelski for nearly two hours in Krakow. Poland's news agency said the meeting was a follow-up to their talks last week. It coincided with the arrival of Lech Walesa, head of the outlawed Solidarity union. The session raised speculation that the three might meet together. Saturday, the pope again met with the government raised by the Roman Catholic leader's eight-day visit might have prompted Gen. Jaruzelski to request the meeting, thus ending martial law.

Jaruzelski's trip to Krakow came after the largest pro-Solidarity rallies since the imposition of martial law.

REAGAN IS STARTING a new effort to help rid Lebanon of foreign troops.

Shultz said U.S. envoy Philip Habib and Morris Draper are returning to the Mideast, probably tomorrow. They have been in the U.S. planning strategy to persuade Syria and the PLO to follow Israel's lead in pledging to withdraw forces. But the secretary of state acknowledged that the diplomatic hurdles have multiplied. Syria refuses to see Habib.

(Story on Page 3)

PLO chairman Arafat moved his headquarters to Tripoli, Lebanon, from Damascus. And a leader of the mutiny against his leadership offered a truce.

THATCHER PLANS to pursue legislative policies from her first term.

The prime minister will ask Parliament to enact limits on Britain's trade unions, denationalize more state-owned industries and grant police some additional powers. Her program also endorses U.S. arms-control policies and the deployment of new nuclear weapons in Europe.

(Story on Page 33)

With a 144-seat majority in the House of Commons, Thatcher's general program is sure to become law in the coming session, which ends in 1988.

Nicaragua denied responsibility for the deaths of two American journalists killed near the Nicaragua-Honduras border. Dial Torgerson of the Los Angeles Times and free-lance photographer Richard Cross were slain Tuesday. Initial wire-service reports that Time magazine's William McWhirter was also slain were erroneous.

A U.S.-Soviet arms-control accord is unlikely this year, according to a forum in West Berlin of multinational weapons-control specialists. Some of the participants predicted this will mean new American majority, probably will be deployed in Europe later this year.

(Story on Page 34)

Andrean's Senate testimony on the role of the MX missile in arms-control talks with the Soviets will cause negotiations more difficult, the former arms-control director said. Gerald Smith, who held the post under Nixon, called Andrean's plea to preserve the MX as a "bargaining chip."

A school-reform panel suggested that businesses help schools develop plans to improve U.S. education and help raise funds to do so. A report by the 45-member panel surveyed many of the suggestions made by a government-sponsored panel in April last year.

(Story on Page 2)

The Clinch River breeder reactor would lose funding after Sept. 30 under a Senate vote. The chamber voted to proceed $14.2 billion for energy and water development projects, $200 million more than what Reagan sought. But he is considered unlikely to veto the bill. *(Story on Page 4)*

Stockholmian called for a revitalized alliance between the government and scientists to better protect the public from the risks of toxic chemicals. But the EPA chief didn't discuss specific regulative changes in his first proper policy speech since taking office four weeks ago. *(Story on Page 5)*

New Jersey's reapportioning of congressional districts was ruled unconstitutional by the Supreme Court. The 5-4 decision said the new districts violate "equal representation for equal numbers of people." The court warned states that they must justify even slight population changes when they redraw congressional districts. *(Story on Page 4)*

Cigarette packages would carry harsh health warnings under a bill passed 15-1 by the Senate Labor and Human Resources panel. The label would read: "Warning: Cigarette smoking causes cancer, emphysema, heart disease; may complicate pregnancy and is addictive." The bill may face a Senate filibuster. *(Story on Page 3)*

The Indian Point 2 nuclear power plant will be out of service for at least five months because of damage to its electric generator unit. Closing of the New York plant doesn't involve the nuclear reactor.

Italy's ailing economy has emerged as a major factor for next week's elections. Due to the fall of Prime Minister Fanfani's coalition, the voting is a year early. Italy's inflation rate exceeds 16% and the jobless rate is about 10%. *(Story on Page 2)*

Donald Nash was sentenced to 100 years in prison for the April 12, 1982, murder of three CBS technicians and a federal witness at a New York pier.

TODAY'S INDEX

Consumer Prices

CONSUMER PRICES rose in May to 297.1 of the 1967 average from 295.5 in April before seasonal adjustment, the Labor Department reports *(See story on Page 2)*

Rostenkowski Finds That the Old Ways Mean Less and Less

House Chairmen Lose Power; Today He Backs Tax Bill That He Considers Unwise

By ROBERT W. MERRY
Staff Reporter of THE WALL STREET JOURNAL

WASHINGTON—He may be a 25-year veteran of Congress, an intimate of presidents and the chairman of a committee that controls the flow of dollars into the U.S. Treasury. But Rep. Dan Rostenkowski—self-described as "Danny Rosty, the big, brash individual from Chicago"—never forgets his city's 32nd Ward, the starting point for his political career.

That was plain in April at the unveiling of his official portrait as Ways and Means Committee chairman. From the 32nd Ward and environs came his wife and daughters, his boyhood buddies, political cronies, his neighborhood priest. Their tributes mingled with those of Vice President George Bush and House Speaker Thomas O'Neill. Emotions were strong.

"It got to be kind of a sentimental thing with me," the 54-year-old chairman recalls. His smartly forceful voice betraying a mood of subdued reflection. A Republican admirer who was there says: "He was pretty misty-eyed, and it was contagious."

No doubt the emotion flowed in part from a realization that the politics of old, practiced by Danny Rostenkowski much of his life, is dying. It is dying in Chicago, where Harold Washington, the new black mayor, has declared war on the Democratic machine that nourished Mr. Rostenkowski's early career. And it is dying in the House, where Today's special-interest politics often interferes with Mr. Rostenkowski's ideas about governing.

'Losing the Battle'

"Danny is an old-school politician struggling to operate in the old-school way," says Rep. Barbara Kennelly of Connecticut, a Democratic member of Ways and Means. "He's losing the battle."

Today Mr. Rostenkowski goes to the House floor to defend a measure he considers essentially unwise and politically futile. Danny's Podert by eager Democratic investment and embraced by Speaker O'Neill. It would place a $100 limit on this year's installment of President Reagan's three-year tax-rate cuts. It strikes generally at upper-income Americans, and many Democrats see it as a way to portray themselves as politically the party of the common man.

Under instructions from House Democratic leaders, Mr. Rostenkowski guided the bill through his committee last week, but his heart wasn't in it. Privately, he suggests to friends that it is merely a political ploy likely to backfire when President Reagan attacks. And he considers the limit on tax cuts in merely a part of a few hours' worth of emotion.

Thus, the old ways continue to Mr. Rostenkowski's political instinct, which are to get things done, to move legislation, to compromise when necessary. On the night of Chicago's longtime Mayor Richard Daley, who ran the city's wildly disparate interests with iron-fisted control, and Rostenkowski seems to see the old ways as a lament.

Both men are dead, their brand of backroom, command politics replaced by something more chaotic, less controllable. Power has flowed to the House committee chairmen and to infernal-group caucuses—Mr. Blacks, Mr. women, even the freshman class. He sees this as part of a broad new balance of political power that has rushed government to its seeming cant.

Complicating the picture is the intensely partisan focal battle pitting Ronald Reagan and his budgetary conservatives against Tip O'Neill and his pugnacious Democrats. Between them, struggling to maintain his old-style ways, is Danny Rostenkowski.

He is a Democrat to the core and has remained ties to Speaker O'Neill, a longtime friend and venue. But he is that he will realize that the speaker—should he win in bid—has to calculate, adding he would put Mr. O'Neill ahead of him. But Mr. Rostenkowski recalls this point with about this ability to deal with the administration, just as he did in producing the 1981 tax bill.

"I'm a Pole," he says. "The Poles are known to be pretty respectful—disciplined family. Clothes! first. It's hard for me to imagine the president doing something that

Please Turn to Page 25, Column 1

Business Bulletin

A Special Background Report On Trends in Industry And Finance

STOCK EXCHANGES suffer a decline in new listings.

Only 23 companies last year—down from 61 in 1981—left the National Association of Securities Dealers' over-the-counter trading system for the American Stock Exchange. 28 companies, down fewer than in 1981, left for the New York Stock Exchange. So far this year, the pace of defections from the over-the-counter market has remained slow. The NASD's fast-growing National Market, with stock quotes like those on exchanges, evidently helps it retain hundreds of stocks that would qualify for exchanges. These include each fast-growing companies as Apple Computer, Intel and MCI Communications.

Are traditional stock exchanges electronics? Some over-the-counter companies've been as William McGowan, chairman of MCI (and an NASD governor), says MCI now, because there are 25 market-makers for its common stock, enjoys a stronger market than it could have on a stock exchange where a single specialist firm handles all trades.

Daily over-the-counter trading volume topped the Big Board's for the first time May 27, largely because more high-volume issues are forgoing exchange listings.

*   *   *

BANKING MACHINES displace few human tellers so far—but this could change. Publicity, at least, many banks say automated tellers aren't eliminating many people's jobs—and aren't likely to. Says a Bank of Virginia spokesman in Richmond: "I can not foresee an ever turning in our lifetime a bank without human tellers." In Los Angeles, a Security Pacific National Bank executive predicts an unspecified decrease in human tellers but adds: "I don't see an end of the teller in the future, ever."

But privately, responding to a survey by Allied Corp.'s Bunker-Ramon unit, 204 bank execs recently mounted a bit more ominous. On average, the bankers expected machines to replace 17 of every 100 tellers in the next three years alone. The survey didn't ask how many more humans might be displaced eventually. In New York, though, Citibank concedes that machines already have replaced all 31 humans who used to run three branches.

*   *   *

EXPENSE-ACCOUNT DINING perks up at some restaurants.

The business crowd thickens again at Orsi and Le Trianon, two fancy San Francisco restaurants. Says Le Trianon's owner: "We're getting back to the 1981 level." 1981 was a good year. "Sales at La Maison d'Or, Cincinnati, after slackening 7% to 8% last year, have bounced about halfway back; many of the customers are businessmen. Expense-account spending is "very slowly creeping back—we have to love the patience of Methuselah the way things are coming back," says Robert Bunciani, a Seattle restaurateur with customers from Boeing and elsewhere.

At least the Seattle restaurant is doing far as gaters; some others are not so Le Muter, Christ Gables. Fla., says sales are running 15% behind last year. The cocktail wines once favored by businessmen "just don't sell anymore," its owner adds. Face-to-face business entertaining is still building at the major oil companies, as well as big suppliers and caterers, are clients of the labor camps.

*   *   *

PAPERLESS PAYING of corporate dividends is pushed at Consolidated Edison Co. New York, but with little success so far. It's year-old electronic-deposit program has done away with about 1% of the checks. The next to offer electronic dividends will be Wachovia Bank, Winston-Salem, N.C.

A HUMAN BODY (of 154 pounds) usually contains $925 worth of cholesterol, $738.50 of fibrinogen, $2,334 of hemoglobin, $4,439.50 of albumin, $20,663 of myoglobin, $19,600 of IgG, and $186,060 of myoglobin, according to a report in the New England Journal of Medicine and to think, we based we were just a few bucks' worth of chemicals.

SEVERAL AIRLINES—United, TWA, American, Eastern, and possibly others—plan to raise 20% discounts on coach travel July 1. This reflects strong bookings for third-quarter travel. Last year, discounts perished all summer.

BICYCLE SALES, after two years of backpedaling, move forward again. Manufacturers' unit sales of bicycles are running about 17% ahead of last year. According to industry figures, at consumer buying drive up can merchandisers replenish inventories Duxwall Alto Stores, Abilene, Kan., says its bicycle sales are about 50% stronger this year. Lechmere, a store in Cambridge, Mass., reports a 30% gain in sales. The recovery is stronger, bike shops say, and cycling, in any case, may be regaining vogue. Freewheeling Bike Store, New Orleans, says many people are switching from commuting to cycling so that "they don't tear up the back and knees."

Nothing approaching a bicycle boom is under way, though, and U.S. makers don't expect to recoup the estimated 35% drop in unit sales suffered last year. Competition for retail space is fierce, and price markdowns are common. "The $200-to-$300 price range is where they're really sliding it out," says Robert Hylen, a merchant in Pittsburgh.

*   *   *

BRIEFS: A Los Angeles company named MotorMessages will sell advertising space on parking meters in St. Louis. . . . Nicotinol International stretches out its annual report to 16 pages, including a one-page glossary and two-page index.

—*JEFFREY A. TANNENBAUM*

Dirty Work

Louisiana Labor Camps Supply 'Warm Bodies' The Oil Business Needs

Laborers Often Earn Little Beyond Debt to a Camp; Life at a Halfway House

Some Citizens Defend System

By GEORGE GETSCHOW
Staff Reporter of THE WALL STREET JOURNAL

MORGAN CITY, La.—In the early 1980s, when labor shortages threatened to stop the expansion of sugar-cane cultivation in this swampy part of southern Louisiana, some European settlers seized the opportunity to strike it rich by selling slaves to the land owners. Soon the slave trade flourished throughout St. Mary Parish. Traders became wealthy plantation owners, and their descendants are still among the socially prominent here.

In the 1970s, a labor shortage again imperiled the expansion of a local industry: the building and servicing of offshore oil-

Second of two articles

drilling rigs. Again local residents responded. Newspaper ads brought jobless out-of-towners streaming into the area, and to house them entrepreneurs turned old buildings into spartan bunkhouses for transients. Thus developed an institution known hereabouts as the labor camp.

In some cases, also, their origins are use the camps only nowadays to the 20th century system.

A job-seeker acquires a debt for lodging and other items as soon as he joins one of the 100 or so labor camps in what is called Louisiana's "oil patch," the heart of the onshore-oil boom. When he goes to work in the oil business. But many who come out the patch stay in debt, lacking other cash to get a few dollars ahead of the game. But to other cases, he is ensnared by the constantly accumulating charges combined with only sporadic job assignments.

No Exit

"So many of those people that come down from the North to better themselves get caught in a web and find it hard to get out," says Bruce Broadway, a state police investigator, Alfred Rumsey, a wage-and-hour official at the U.S. Labor Department whose agency has sued several labor camps, says that all too frequently "the camps take all the money and the workers wind up with nothing."

Despite the hazards of generalizing it can be said that both men's impressions were confirmed in a four-month investigation by this newspaper.

Twenty-four hours a day, seven days a week, the offshore oil industry needs a supply of roustabouts, dishwashers and other largely unskilled laborers. "Warm bodies" is the universal term for them here in Morgan City, the mainland headquarters for offshore drilling. Shell Oil, Mobil, Texaco, Kerr-McGee and nearly all the major oil companies, as well as big suppliers and caterers, are clients of the labor camps.

Pillars of Community

Many of the owners are prominent local people. They include businessmen, elected officials, deputy sheriffs, physicians and a churchman or two. C.H. Brownell, who was Morgan City's mayor until this week and used labor-camp residents as garbage collectors and for other work, employs the town's trickling this way: "The camps serve a legitimate need; it's just that some undesirables have given them a bad name."

The operators do not call their places labor camps. One, for instance, is known as the St. Mary Council on Alcoholism & Drug Abuse. It was started 13 years ago as a non-profit rehabilitation center and now includes a halfway house. Directors include a state senator, a physician and ex-mayor, an operator, a design sheriff and a former superintendent of education.

But the boss at the halfway house is John Curl, a six-foot-five, 240-pound ex-convict who many former camp residents say curries a derringer in his big pocket. He denies having any boots or any firearms but his, saying, "Everybody's afraid of him," says Robert Morgan, who until recently lived at the halfway house. "I've stood them and watched him beat people up and been too scared to do anything." "That's not true," Mr. Curl replies. "We're the ones who get beat up."

Sheriff's Commission

Despite his criminal record, Mr. Curl holds a St. Mary Parish sheriff's commission. And the sheriff's department has been helpful to him and the labor camp. Every week, sheriff's deputies deliver men to the halfway house. "We do it to give these people an opportunity to get a job after we transport a place to stay," says Deputy Sheriff Daryl Arthur. "We don't have a drunk-tank facility."

But Thor Helms, who served refuge at the halfway house two years ago, says drunkenness sometimes has nothing to do with being in the camp. He was roundly at the St. Mary Parish jail on a "simple stream of alcoholic drinks and sedative drugs that kept him in "a hypnotic state." After 11 days, he continues, Mr. Curl bailed him out of jail and took him to a labor camp disguised as a drug-treatment center called Oceanic Bar.

At the time, according to Mr. Helms and several other former workers, Mr. Curl had an arrangement with two of Oceanic Bar's personnel officers in exchange for cash payments, they would use laborers from the St. Mary Council halfway house—an obligation the men's attorneys say is a debt-bondage arrangement "could be a scheme of the men's paycheck to be their own bail to

Please Turn to Page 12, Column 1

Pulitzer Prizes for editorial writing and reporting.

Among the Dow Jones Company's many innovations was the launching of a general weekly, the *National Observer,* in 1962. It had a circulation of more than five hundred thousand, but finally died in 1977 because of advertising problems.

Using satellite transmission of its pages made in New York, the *Wall Street Journal* was producing four essentially similar editions in seventeen printing plants by 1983. It had passed the *Daily News* in circulation by 1980 and was near the two million mark. Warren Phillips was board chairman for Dow Jones, and two onetime reporters, Peter Kann and Edward Cony, were vice-presidents in the news area. Robert L. Bartley, 1980 Pulitzer Prize winner for editorial writing, was editor, while the newest managing editor was Norm Pearlstine.

The paper had twenty-five news bureaus, eleven abroad. Its Washington bureau, second only to that of the *New York Times,* had as top correspondents James M. Perry and Albert R. Hunt in politics and Karen Elliott House in foreign affairs. The *Asian Wall Street Journal* began publishing in 1976 and in 1983 the *Wall Street Journal/Europe* entered the international competition. The AP-Dow Jones News Service covered forty countries with economic news.

The Washington Post

The survey results showed that the *Washington Post* and *Wall Street Journal* battled for positions two and three in nearly every region, with the *Los Angeles Times* close behind the *Post*. Overall the *Post* emerged with the most support for the third position, not a surprising conclusion when one considers the vast amount of publicity the paper received a decade ago during the Watergate period and continues to receive because of its location. The *Post* has "celebrity" status, along with some of its editors and reporters.

Even in region nine, the Far West, the *Post* earned almost exactly the same number of points as the regional favorite, the *Los Angeles Times*. The rankings for the "top 5" in that region showed the *New York Times* far ahead with 388 points (based on a one-to-five point system), the *Post* with 250, the *Los Angeles Times* with 249, and the *Wall Street Journal* with 222. Throughout the nation the Washington paper edged its Los Angeles rival (the papers share a supplementary news service) by enough responses to earn the third spot, although it could not overcome the national strength of the *Wall Street Journal*.

Eugene Meyer, a civic-minded Washingtonian who had succeeded in the financial world, rescued the *Post* from receivership in 1933. Meyer

Weather

Today—Sunny and warm, high in the upper 80s and low 90s, fair tonight, low in upper 60s and low 70s. Friday—Sunny, high in the upper 80s and low 90s. Yesterday—4 p.m. AQI: 65; temperature range: 83-68. Details, B2.

The Washington Post

Index 104 Pages 8 Sections

Classified	B 8	Movies	D13
Comics	C21	Obituaries	B 6
Editorials	A22	Sports	C 1
Federal Diary	B 2	Style	D 1
Financial	C10	Style Plus	D 5
Metro	B 1	Television	D12

Inside: Washington Ho—

106th Year · No. 200 © 1983, The Washington Post Company THURSDAY, JUNE 23, 1983 Higher in Areas Approximately 75 miles From District of Columbia (See Box on A3) G

Satellite Pickup Succeeds

By Thomas O'Toole
Washington Post Staff Writer

CAPE CANAVERAL, June 22—The Challenger astronauts scored another major first today when they launched a satellite and flew in formation with it for six Earth orbits while repeatedly retrieving it with a mechanical arm and finally returning it to the space shuttle's cargo bay.

Astronauts Robert L. Crippen, Frederick H. Hauck, John M. Fabian, Sally K. Ride and Norman E. Thagard flew in formation for eight hours with a satellite built by a West German aerospace company, Messerschmitt-Bolkow-Blohm, while cameras aboard Challenger and the German satellite recorded the spectacular exercise on film.

Carried out 180 miles above the Earth, the maneuvers were no mere exercise in space. The astronauts were, in fact, rehearsing for the 13th space shuttle flight late next year. Its crew will retrieve a damaged satellite called the Solar Maximum Mission, pull it back into the cargo bay, repair it and put it back to work in space again.

Looking for all the world like a flying bedstead or a wrecked car in orbit, the 15-foot-long German satellite was lifted out of the cargo bay with the shuttle's 50-foot-long mechanical arm and let go in space just after 3 a.m. More than 10 hours later, astronauts Fabian and Ride used the mechanical arm to haul the 3,200-pound satellite back from space a final time and lock it up inside the cargo bay.

Though the astronauts are still scheduled to return to earth Friday and make the first spacecraft land-

See SHUTTLE, A7, Col. 1

Associated Press

Challenger as seen from the television camera of the West German scientific satellite that was launched from the shuttle.

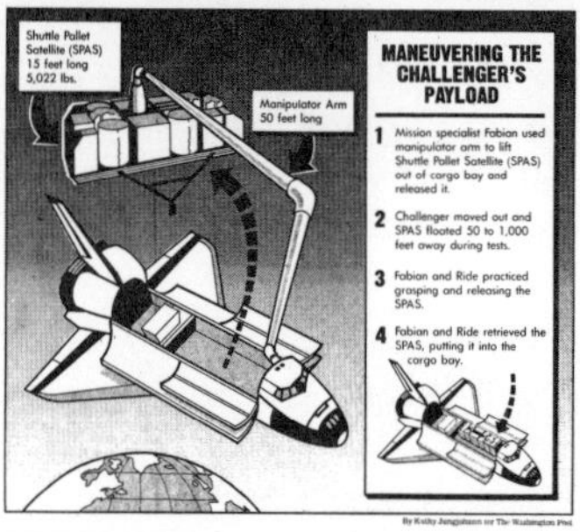
Shuttle Pallet Satellite (SPAS) 15 feet long 5,022 lbs.
Manipulator Arm 50 feet long
MANEUVERING THE CHALLENGER'S PAYLOAD
1 Mission specialist Fabian used manipulator arm to lift Shuttle Pallet Satellite (SPAS) out of cargo bay and released it.
2 Challenger moved out and SPAS floated 50 to 1,000 feet away during tests.
3 Fabian and Ride practiced grasping and releasing the SPAS.
4 Fabian and Ride retrieved the SPAS, putting it into the cargo bay.

By Kathy Jungjohann for The Washington Post

U.S. Laying Plans For Talking With Salvadoran Rebels

By John M. Goshko and Joanne Omang
Washington Post Staff Writers

Reagan administration officials, while publicly opposing negotiations that would give El Salvador's leftist guerrillas a share of governmental power, are moving quietly toward talks with the insurgents aimed at inducing them to stop fighting and take part in planned elections, informed sources said yesterday.

The effort, still being planned, reportedly differs from past U.S. approaches couched in bellicose rhetoric about not permitting the guerrillas "to shoot their way into power" and that focused exclusively on calls for them to lay down their arms.

Now, the administration, working secretly through various diplomatic contacts, is allegedly trying for a more broadly based agenda that would satisfy some of the leftists' demands and concerns, permit U.S. mediation between government and insurgents and lead ultimately to at least part of the left joining the electoral process.

Reports of the effort come as the administration prepares to certify to Congress that progress has been made in El Salvador toward guaranteeing human rights and reaching a political settlement, a requirement imposed as a condition for approving further military aid.

For that reason, and because of extreme secrecy surrounding the situation, it was not immediately clear whether administration officials believe the move has a real chance of success or is essentially a tactic to pacify congressional critics.

Suggestions of any move toward power-sharing negotiations have been disavowed strongly by President Reagan and key policy-makers such as national security affairs adviser William P. Clark. However, the sources said, the current effort has been approved by top officials formerly in conflict.

At a news conference yesterday, Secretary of State George P. Shultz hinted at the administration's direction in noting that the peace commission established by the U.S.-backed Salvadoran government "has stated its willingness to discuss with the left the conditions under which they might enter the political process."

Shultz added that if the United

See LATIN, A19, Col. 1

GEORGE P. SHULTZ
... "We continue to be fully engaged"

2 U.S. Mideast Troubleshooters Will Try Again

By Don Oberdorfer
Washington Post Staff Writer

Secretary of State George P. Shultz announced yesterday that U.S. troubleshooters Philip C. Habib and Morris Draper are undertaking another Middle East mission this week but there was no indication of a break in the logjam over the withdrawal of Syrian forces from Lebanon.

"We continue to be fully engaged" in efforts to bring about the withdrawal of all foreign forces from Lebanon, Shultz told a news conference. He conceded, though, that "the problems are real," especially Syria's refusal under present circumstances to pull out its troops.

Syria declined in mid-May to accept a visit from Habib, a refusal that stands as a limiting factor on the veteran diplomat's usefulness in the current situation. Because of the Syrian position, Habib "won't go" to Damascus, Shultz said, "and we will find other people who we hope will be acceptable to them."

The secretary gave no hint who the substitute emissary might be. Another official said planning is "not far along" on a new approach to the Syrians.

See SHULTZ, A30, Col. 1

Pope, Jaruzelski Hold Unexpected Second Meeting

By Bradley Graham
Washington Post Foreign Service

KRAKOW, Poland, June 22—Pope John Paul II today held an unexpected second meeting with Polish leader Gen. Wojciech Jaruzelski here at the end of a day that saw the largest pro-Solidarity demonstration since military rule was imposed 18 months ago.

The meeting in this southern Polish city—which the pope is scheduled to leave Thursday as he departs for Rome—lasted two hours and Polish television said it had been called at the request of the Vatican.

The official Polish press agency described the session as a continuation of talks held by the two leaders in Warsaw on Friday, the day after the pope arrived in Poland, and made only indirect reference to the church-state tensions that have increased during the week-long papal pilgrimage. The Polish statement said:

"The hope was expressed that the visit will contribute to the peaceful and favorable development of social life in Poland and the strengthening of peace in Europe and in the world. It was also recognized that further contact between the apostolic see and the Polish United Workers [Communist] Party will serve the good of the state and the church."

[Thousands of Poles outside the archbishop's residence in Krakow spotted the pope at a window after the meeting with Jaruzelski at the Wawel Castle and shouted, "What happened at the castle?" The Associated Press reported. The pope smiled and replied, "You should have been at the castle."]

Meanwhile, on a day that saw the biggest crowds of the pope's visit—ranging up to 2 million for an outdoor mass—Lech Walesa, the leader of the outlawed Solidarity trade union, accompanied by his wife Danuta and four children, arrived here tonight for a meeting Thursday with the pope, who reserved his final day in Poland for a private program.

See POPE, A26, Col. 1

D.C. Students Increase Scores Dramatically

By Ronald D. White
Washington Post Staff Writer

District public school students increased their scores dramatically on comprehensive standardized tests this spring, indicating a continuing improvement in the six skills that were tested, school officials said yesterday.

Sixth grade students surpassed national norms in five of six skill areas for the first time since the schools began systemwide testing five years ago, officials said yesterday.

Third grade students, who surpassed national norms in math, science, language and reference skills for the first time last year, continued to improve this year, exceeding national norms in those areas and also in reading and social studies.

In the past, test scores in the District have fallen far below national standards. Ninth and 11th grade students still fell short of the national norms this year but showed substantial improvement over last year in each of the six skills tested: reading, math, language, reference skills, science and social studies. Eleventh graders showed the most dramatic improvement, although their scores were still below the national norms.

Only students in grades 3, 6, 9 and 11 were tested.

"These test data indicate the continued academic progress of all of our students," D.C. School Superintendent Floretta D. McKenzie said at a press conference announcing the scores yesterday. "The results are very gratifying." School board president David Eaton added: "I'm tremendously pleased with this report."

Saying that the improved scores were "a direct reflection of the de-

See SCHOOLS, A8, Col. 3

Nicaragua, Honduras Dispute Newsmen's Deaths

By Edward Cody
Washington Post Foreign Service

TEGUCIGALPA, Honduras, June 22—A Honduran Army helicopter flew the bodies of two slain American journalists to Tegucigalpa for shipment home today as the Nicaraguan government rejected charges that fire from its soldiers killed the reporters as they drove along the Honduran side of the embattled border yesterday.

Dial Torgerson, 55, of the Los Angeles Times and Richard Cross, 33, a free-lance photographer on assignment for U.S. News and World Report, were the first American journalists killed in the expanding war in southern Honduras. [Obituary on Page B6.]

Their white four-door Toyota sedan was destroyed yesterday afternoon by a rocket-propelled grenade that Honduran and U.S. authorities said was fired by Sandinista soldiers from within nearby Nicaraguan territory.

A third man, originally said to have been the driver of the journalists' car, today was identified as a Honduran civilian who was walking near the car when it exploded. According to a Honduran military spokesman, the man, Jose Hererra Rodriquez, 27, was severely wounded by the force of the explosion and was operated on in Tegucigalpa this afternoon.

The Nicaraguan Foreign Ministry, in a statement issued in Managua, denied the Honduran charge. It said no Sandinista soldiers fired into Honduran territory, and depicted the journalists as "victims of the criminal violence that the United States government has unleashed in Central America, particularly along the Nicaraguan-Honduran border."

[In Washington, Secretary of State George P. Shultz said "the fire" that killed the two newsmen "did come from Nicaragua." A State Department spokesman said that "we will, through our embassy in Mana-

See JOURNALISTS, A18, Col. 1

High Court Tightens Redistricting Rules

By Fred Barbash
Washington Post Staff Writer

A divided Supreme Court tightened its one-man, one-vote rule yesterday, saying population differences of less than a single percentage point among congressional districts in a state may be unconstitutional.

The dissenting justices said the new standard could lead to irrationally drawn districts and actually more gerrymandering by state legislatures, not less.

The 5-to-4 ruling declared New Jersey's 1982 redistricting plan unconstitutional because its largest congressional district has 3,674 more people than the smallest—a deviation of about one seventh of 1 percent from absolute equality. The court said the state can bring about even greater equality.

The decision raised legal questions about plans in at least 16 states, including Virginia, which have deviations larger or about the same as New Jersey's.

The ruling does not mean these plans are necessarily invalid. But if court challenges demonstrate that greater equality was feasible, the states must then assume the heavy burden of offering specific, legitimate policy justifications for retaining their plans, the court said.

The opinion, written by Justice William J. Brennan Jr., guaranteed an even greater future role in the redistricting process for the federal courts, which many politicians think are already exercising too much authority. It imposed new levels of mathematical precision on state

See REDISTRICTING, A14, Col. 1

Consumer Prices Rise 0.5% in May

The Consumer Price Index rose 0.5 percent in May, pushed largely by higher gasoline costs, the Labor Department reported yesterday. It was the second sharp monthly increase in a row, but most economists expect inflation to be in the 3-4 percent range for 1983.

Details on Page C10

Breeder Reactor Dealt New Blow

The Clinch River breeder reactor yesterday suffered a potentially lethal blow as the Senate joined the House in voting to block further work on the controversial nuclear power project until a new financing arrangement can be worked out by the Department of Energy.

Details on Page A6

AMA Votes to Fight Dioxin 'Witch Hunt'

By Philip J. Hilts
Washington Post Staff Writer

The American Medical Association accused the news media yesterday of conducting a "witch hunt" against the toxic chemical dioxin, and decided to mount a public relations campaign to counter the "hysteria."

By voice vote, its 351-member House of Delegates decided in Chicago that the AMA will adopt "an active public information campaign . . . to prevent irrational reaction and unjustified public fright and to prevent the dissemination of possibly erroneous information" about the health hazards of dioxin.

Dr. George Bohigian, a member of the AMA council on scientific affairs and sponsor of the resolution, said that no serious medical effects on humans have been found to have resulted from the dioxin accidents and spills studied over the past two decades.

Bohigian said that medical reports, including a 1981 AMA survey, have found only two short-term effects of dioxin on humans. One is a skin condition called chloracne, which is similar to severe acne. The other is apparently temporary nerve damage that causes numbness and similar effects.

Bohigian is an opthalmologist at Washington University in St. Louis, in a state with some of the nation's worst dioxin contamination.

Meanwhile, an editorial in the current issue of Science magazine, published by the American Association for the

See DIOXIN, A5, Col. 1

Syrians Encircle PLO Positions In East Lebanon

By Herbert H. Denton
Washington Post Foreign Service

BAALBEK, Lebanon, June 22—Syrian soldiers encircled Palestine Liberation Organization positions in eastern Lebanon today, forbidding movements of guerrillas loyal to PLO Chairman Yasser Arafat and turning away shipments of arms and ammunition to them.

Rebels claimed yesterday that they had taken eight strategic PLO positions in the Bekaa Valley. Two key aides to Arafat disputed that today, however, saying the rebels had captured only two to four positions, but they claimed that after the battle yesterday, Syrians increased their checkpoints around PLO positions in eastern Lebanon and installed dissidents to man checkpoints along the road in the area.

"We're still in the Bekaa," said Ahmed Abdel Rahman, Arafat's chief spokesman. "We're still in Baalbek, but they took the roads."

The PLO military chief, Khalil Wazir, known as Abu Jihad, said rebels helped the Syrians in identifying Arafat loyalists and routinely disarmed them today if they attempted to move from their positions.

He said that the Syrians were permitting food to pass through their lines but either seized or turned away arms and military cargo intended for the loyalists.

Today's developments complicated further the situation within the PLO, where elements of Arafat's main Fatah organization have launched a challenge to Arafat's leadership, saying he is leading the guerrilla movement away from its main goal of confronting Israel.

The reining in of the PLO appeared to strengthen the bargaining

See PLO, A30, Col. 1

wanted his city to have a paper with sound editorial page leadership, and he was successful there as well. Two editorial page editors, Felix Morey, who served until 1940, and Herbert Elliston, who was in the position until 1953, won Pulitzer Prizes for their work. The cartoons of Herbert L. Block (Herblock) gave the page added distinction. The *Post* soon was known as the most independent paper in the capital and it also carried a heavy volume of foreign news.

Meyer became president of the International Bank in 1946, naming his son-in-law, Philip L. Graham, as publisher. The *Post* purchased its morning competition, the *Times-Herald,* in 1954. With James Russell Wiggins as editor and Alfred Friendly as managing editor, the *Post* urged improved journalistic practices and strongly defended First Amendment freedoms. The paper gained attention during its long battle with Wisconsin Senator Joseph R. McCarthy and Vice-President Richard Nixon. Both men were the frequent targets of Herblock's pen. Politically the paper avoided endorsements, but favored the candidacies of Dewey, Eisenhower and Kennedy.

Katharine Graham assumed control of the Washington Post Company following her husband's suicide in 1963. *Newsweek* and television stations were part of the holdings.

Mrs. Graham's decision to make Benjamin C. Bradlee managing editor in 1966—and later executive editor—paved the way for a number of exciting developments at the *Post.* Howard Simons took Bradlee's place as managing editor. In the 1970s the paper took center stage during the Watergate crisis as Bradlee, Simons, and others guided the reporting of Carl Bernstein and Bob Woodward, despite threats from the Nixon White House. The *Post* won the Pulitzer Prize and enormous international prestige. The *Post* had finally caught the *New York Times* in the battle for Washington coverage.

Editorial page editors Philip Geyelin and Meg Greenfield—both Pulitzer Prize winners—helped shape the paper's image as a leader among liberal-intellectual newspapers, as did columnists David Broder and Nicholas Von Hoffman.

Donald Graham, thirty-four-year-old son of the Grahams, was named publisher of the *Post* in 1979, while his mother continued to head the company operations and served as first woman president of the American Newspaper Publishers Association. Karen DeYoung, prize-winning Latin American correspondent, became foreign editor. The *Post's* handling of a 1981 episode involving a Pulitzer Prize article which proved fictitious, and its loss of a major libel suit, drew criticism in media circles, but the *Post* recouped with two 1983 Pulitzer awards. The *Post's* 1983 circulation was 747,000 on weekdays.

Los Angeles Times

Circulation: 1,072,500 Daily / 1,358,420 Sunday — Thursday, June 23, 1983 — CC†/180 pages / Copyright 1983, Los Angeles Times / Daily 25¢

Patient-Therapist

Risk vs. Duty in Warning of Violence

By JOAN SWEENEY, *Times Human Behavior Writer*

Some California psychotherapists fear that a new federal appellate court decision places them in a Catch-22 situation: On one hand they risk being sued for failing to warn a potential victim of a dangerous patient; but if they do issue such a warning, they risk being sued for breaking a patient's confidentiality.

The opinion by the U.S. 9th Circuit Court of Appeals last week said that Loma Linda Veterans Administration psychiatrists evaluating Phillip Jablonski should have warned his lover, Melinda Kimball, whom he subsequently murdered, that she was a likely target of his violence, even though he had made no threat against her.

This ruling expanded the California Supreme Court's landmark 1974 Tarasoff decision, which held that psychotherapists have a legal duty to warn intended victims of a dangerous patient who had made a specific threat against them. In 1976, the court altered its decision, saying that when such a patient made a threat against another person, the psychotherapist was required to take "reasonable care" to protect the person.

'Reasonably Necessary'

At that time, the court said that, depending on the case, the therapist might warn the intended victim or others who would be likely to tell the victim of the danger, notify the police "or take whatever other steps are reasonably necessary under the circumstances."

In the Jablonski ruling, which upheld a $282,000 malpractice award, the Circuit Court said, "Unlike the killer in Tarasoff, Jablonski made no specific threats concerning any specific individuals. Nevertheless, Jablonski's previous history indicated that he would likely direct his violence against Kimball. He had raped and committed other acts of violence against his previous wife. His psychological profile indicated that his violence was likely to be directed against women very close to him."

'Consequences Dreadful'

The Tarasoff decision generated considerable anxiety among mental health professionals, and the new decision by the circuit court is likely to add to it. The concern stems not only from the increased liability and from the conflicting legal requirement that information acquired in treating patients be kept confidential, but from the difficulty of predicting future violence, the destructive effect this may have on the therapy, and confusion over whom the ruling applies to and what constitutes a warning.

"The 9th Circuit has drastically, catastrophically broadened Tarasoff," said Dr. Thomas K. Ciesla, chairman of the psychiatry department at St. John's Hospital in Santa Monica. "The consequences of not predicting on either side are dreadful to contemplate."

If one errs in the direction of warning everybody who might possibly be in danger from a patient, then there is a massive intrusion on civil rights, Ciesla contended. "But if one errs in the direction of not being vigorous enough in ferreting

Please see WARNING, Page 22

Shuttle Climaxes Flight by Satellite Pickup, Delivery

By RUDY ABRAMSON, *Times Staff Writer*

CAPE CANAVERAL—The five astronauts aboard the spaceship Challenger demonstrated Wednesday that the space shuttle can intercept and recover damaged satellites in orbit and bring them back to Earth for repairs.

Writing a perfect climax to their six-day flight, they freed a satellite the size of a mid-size sedan from the spacecraft's cargo bay, then played cat and mouse with it for 10½ hours before stowing it away for the trip home.

It marked the first time an orbiting satellite had been recovered in space, and gave the National Aeronautics and Space Administration confidence that it can carry through next year with a plan to repair a dead solar satellite now circling the Earth.

"I've been told that some crews in

Please see SHUTTLE, Page 8

House Approves $127.5 Million for L.A. Subway

By ELLEN HUME, *Times Staff Writer*

WASHINGTON—Los Angeles' first major subway, the 18.6-mile Metro Rail project linking downtown with the San Fernando Valley, cleared its toughest congressional hurdle Wednesday when the House approved $127.5 million to begin construction in June, 1984.

A last-minute telegram to congressional leaders from Gov. George Deukmejian apparently helped sway the House to vote, 280 to 139, against an amendment by Rep. Bobbi Fiedler (R-Northridge) to delete the money from the 1984 Department of Transportation appropriations bill.

The $11.3-billion bill, approved 250 to 156 Wednesday, would also provide funds for federal highways, airport development grants, the Coast Guard and Amtrak. The measure includes $30 million for a new Santa Clara County light-rail system, $8.3 million for the San Diego trolley, more than $4 million for microwave landing systems at Los Angeles International Airport and restrictions on spending federal funds for a new terminal at Burbank Airport until a noise compatibility master plan is developed.

4 Californians in Opposition

Fiedler was joined in opposition to subway funding by only three other Californians—fellow Republicans Dan Lungren (Long Beach) and Robert E. Badham (Newport Beach) and liberal Democrat Fortney H. Stark (Oakland), who said he was getting even with Los Angeles for "stealing the Oakland Raiders" football team.

Because the subway is favored by Sens. Pete Wilson (R-Calif.) and Alan Cranston (D-Calif.), as well as by Gov. Deukmejian, the Los Angeles County Board of Supervisors, the City Council and the Los Angeles Area Chamber of Commerce, the funding measure is expected to sail easily through the Senate. The Reagan Administration does not oppose the new subway, whose

Please see SUBWAY, Page 3

Associated Press

The dirt road in Honduras on which two journalists were killed; at this point the Nicaragua border is about 100 yards to the left.

Torgerson Died While Doing Job

Road Led to a Nowhere Village—and to Death

By WILLIAM D. MONTALBANO, *Times Staff Writer*

TEGUCIGALPA, Honduras—Dial Torgerson, newspaperman, died doing his job.

Tuesday, Times correspondent Torgerson and free-lance photographer Richard Cross drove down a dirt track to a nowhere village on the Nicaraguan border called Las Trojes. On the way back out, they died.

Torgerson and Cross had no chance.

Eyewitnesses say their car was struck at window level by a rocket-propelled grenade, an anti-tank weapon. Then it was raked by long bursts of machine-gun fire that wounded a passing peasant.

The witnesses said Wednesday that the fire had come from inside

Related stories and photos on Page 11, 12, 15 and 16.

Nicaragua. Honduras and the United States accused the Nicaraguan armed forces of the killing.

In Managua on Wednesday, the Nicaraguan Foreign Ministry denied the accusation. In a statement, it rejected the "false accusation made by the government of Honduras," and called the journalists "victims of the criminal violence that the United States government has unleashed in Central America, particularly along the Nicaraguan-Honduran border."

The bodies of Torgerson, the 55-year-old Mexico City bureau chief for The Times, and Cross, 33, a Los Angeles photographer taking pictures for both The Times and U.S. News and World Report, were returned to the United States on Wednesday night for funeral services.

Torgerson and Cross had casually joined forces here Monday in what was to become their last assignment.

A cautious professional with a puckish sense of humor and a fascination for the Central American turmoil he had covered for the past few years, Torgerson especially liked Tegucigalpa. He was married here last August to Lynda Schuster, a Wall Street Journal correspondent now also based in Mexico City.

This week, Torgerson came to Honduras for a story about the border war that is raging between Nicaraguan armed forces and U.S.-sponsored guerrillas, universally known in Spanish shorthand as contras. The Times had planned to pair Torgerson's story from Honduras on the counterrevolution with one written on its impact inside Nicaragua.

"You do a thousand words from Managua, and I'll do a thousand from Te-Goose (Tegucigalpa) and

Please see NEWSMEN, Page 16

Arafat Trying to Salvage His Role in PLO

By J. MICHAEL KENNEDY, *Times Staff Writer*

BEIRUT—Yasser Arafat, head of the Palestine Liberation Organization, on Wednesday sat in the northern Lebanese port city of Tripoli, his new headquarters, desperately trying to find a way to salvage his once-unquestioned leadership of the guerrilla movement.

But since Tuesday, Arab analysts here said, Arafat has entered into a kind of self-imposed isolation that could mark the beginning of a diminished role for him as PLO leader.

Arafat's immediate problem is a six-week-old mutiny within Fatah, his own guerrilla faction within the PLO. In fighting Tuesday, Arafat's supporters in Fatah lost eight key positions to the mutineers along the Beirut-Damascus highway in eastern Lebanon. Because a portion of the road was in rebel hands, Arafat was forced to take a circuitous route from Damascus to Tripoli.

And, once there, he said publicly

Please see PLO, Page 18

Pope Meets With Poland's Leader

Special Session Sought by Regime Follows Mass Solidarity Protest

By DAN FISHER and DON A. SCHANCHE, *Times Staff Writers*

KRAKOW, Poland—Pope John Paul II held a surprise one-hour, 40-minute meeting with Poland's leader, Gen. Wojciech Jaruzelski, on Wednesday night shortly after his appearances here inspired the largest pro-Solidarity demonstrations since the declaration of martial law in December, 1981.

The two events were not directly connected, although tension between the Pope and the government has been steadily increasing ever since he arrived a week ago and began a series of uncompromising calls for freedom and human rights.

A government source said the meeting had been held at the request of church authorities. However, it is known that Jaruzelski, who met the pontiff with aides last Friday, had wanted a man-to-man session from early in the negotiations that preceded the papal visit.

Church-State Relations

The source said that Wednesday's talks followed several days of negotiations. He said he believes that the discussions centered on the future of church-state relations in Poland and the possibility of establishing full diplomatic ties with the Vatican.

A few miles away from the meeting site in Krakow's historic Wawel Castle, an estimated 50,000 demonstrators marched under dozens of Solidarity banners through the streets of Nowa Huta after an outdoor service at which the pontiff dedicated a new church in the Krakow suburb.

Some of the marchers had earlier participated in smaller demonstrations after an outdoor papal Mass attended by an estimated 2 million faithful who blanketed the vast Krakow meadows in the city center.

Chanting "No freedom without Solidarity!" and "End martial law!" the mostly young marchers finally dispersed when confronted by more than 100 trucks and vans loaded with riot police who blocked the main road between the steel-making suburb and central Krakow. The demonstrators had intended to walk the five miles into the city center to join the vast throngs around the archbishop's residence where John Paul is staying.

"We don't want to disrupt the visit of the distinguished Pope," a senior police officer reasoned over a police car's loudspeaker.

Still, the last of the demonstrators did not disperse until requested to do so by a priest who was sent to the scene after negotiations between the authorities and Krakow church officials.

Relaxed, Enjoying Himself

Despite his hectic schedule on the last full day of his pilgrimage, the pontiff appeared to be relaxed and enjoying himself in this city that he served for 20 years as bishop and cardinal.

In his remarks Wednesday, the Pope was less forthright than he had been, but subtly wove in the same themes of nationalism and resistance to oppression that he had developed in earlier, blunter speeches. For example, at his gigantic outdoor Mass in the Krakow meadows, the pontiff beatified two Polish monks—Father Rafal Kalinowski and Brother Albert Chmielowski—both famous for their participation in an 1863 uprising against the Russians. One was mutilated and the other sent to a Siberian salt mine.

'Love of Homeland'

"Both were inspired by heroic love of the homeland," John Paul said.

His most pointed remarks, again referring to the beatified monks, stressed that their strength was "more powerful than any human weakness and more powerful than any situation, even the most difficult, not excluding the arrogant use

Please see TALKS, Page 17

Ruling Jeopardizes Validity of Reapportionment Plans

By JIM MANN, *Times Staff Writer*

WASHINGTON—In an action that clouds the validity of many of the congressional reapportionment plans carried out after the 1980 census, the Supreme Court ruled 5 to 4 Wednesday that its "one-man, one-vote" decision requires states to try to wipe out even the tiniest variances in population between one district and another.

The high court struck down as unconstitutional a reapportionment plan for New Jersey in which the largest of the state's 14 congressional districts differed from the smallest by 3,674 people. That figure represented a mere 0.6984% of the population of the average congressional district in the state—526,059, according to the latest census figures.

New Jersey legislative officials had pointed out that that difference was below the expected undercount of population in the 1980 census for the New Jersey districts and was so small as to be insignificant. The four justices who dissented Wednesday agreed and upbraided the majority for what they called an "unreasonable insistence on an unattainable perfection in the equalizing of congressional districts."

But the court dismissed those complaints, saying that New Jersey's reapportionment plan violated prior decisions requiring that "as nearly as is practicable," congressional districts must be drawn in a way that equalizes population.

"Adopting any standard other than population equality, using the best census data available, would subtly erode the Constitution's ideal of equal representation," wrote Justice William J. Brennan Jr., the court's senior member, who in 1962 wrote the landmark ruling granting federal courts the power to decide

Please see COURT, Page 10

Growing Older in America

Football's Deacon Jones: 'I Have to Be Top Banana'

By JERRY COHEN, *Times Staff Writer*

David (Deacon) Jones, community relations officer for a Los Angeles brewery, is considered by many to be the greatest defensive end ever to play professional football. As a member of the Los Angeles Rams' "Fearsome Foursome" in the '60s and early '70s, he was known as "the secretary of defense." He was 10 times an All-Pro selection and twice the National Football League's defensive player of the year. He is a huge, solid man with soft brown eyes and a mustache and an outgoing manner. At the time of this conversation, he was 41 and had been retired from football for five years and had just been elected to Professional Football's Hall of Fame.

This is another in a series about growing older in today's America. Not old. Merely older. These reports derive from conversations conducted over a year-long period. The subjects' age and circumstances are the ones that prevailed at the time of the interviews.

To be frank and positive and honest with you, (chronological) age did not drive me out of football. It's just that I got to the point where I couldn't perform the way I like to perform. I couldn't dominate.

I could have played. I could have been a better-than-average player. But that isn't good enough for me. So it was time for me to step aside. I realized that I didn't have to have that beat into my brains before I accepted it.

See, because I am a professional, I have to be the top banana. And you don't reign supreme in professional

Please see JONES, Page 20

INDEX

WEATHER

U.S. Weather Service forecast: Today through Friday—late night through mid-morning low clouds, otherwise fair.

	Highs	Lows
Wednesday	81	60
Today's forecast	mid-80s	mid-60s
Friday's forecast	mid-80s	near 65
June 22 last year	72	60
Record high June 22, 1949	97	
Record low June 22, 1885		51

Complete details, Part IV, Page 15.

New Appeal Court Decision Affirms Drunk Driving Law

By PHILIP HAGER, *Times Staff Writer*

SAN FRANCISCO—A state Court of Appeal panel Wednesday upheld California's new "get-tough" blood-alcohol limit for drunk driving, disagreeing with a controversial finding by another appellate panel that the provision is unconstitutional.

The new ruling, rendered in a unanimous opinion by the three-member panel, set the stage for a review of the law by the state Supreme Court. It is up to that court to resolve conflicts between appellate courts.

The law, imposed in 1982 in a wave of concern over drunk driving, made it illegal to drive with a blood-alcohol level of .10% or more.

On June 2, an appellate panel here ruled 2 to 1 that the measure is unconstitutionally vague, failing to provide the drinking driver with a "reasonably ascertainable means of knowing" when his own level of consumption has reached the allowable limit.

The ruling set off a storm of protest. Appellate Justice William A. Newsom, who joined with Appellate Justice John T. Racanelli to form the court majority, said afterward he received a "deluge" of angry phone calls and letters. Attending a Little League baseball game with his son, Newsom was screamed at by an irate woman as a "goddamned idiot."

Last week, state Atty. Gen. John Van de Kamp, noting that 23 other states and at least 20 countries have enacted similar statutes, urged the panel to reconsider its decision. Van de Kamp, pointing out that nearly half of the 23,000 fatal accidents in California in a five-year period involved alcohol, said that drunk drivers were "cutting a wide swath of death" on the state's high-

Please see COURT, Page 19

The Los Angeles Times

A detailed breakdown of the survey results shows that the nation's largest newspaper, the *Los Angeles Times,* enjoys tremendous support in every section of the nation. The *Times* ranked fourth in eight of the nine regions in the "top 5" ranking, coming in third in its own Far West region. In the "top 10" ratings the *Times* was fourth in five regions, tied for third and fourth twice, and headed the list in its own region nine, by one ballot over the *Wall Street Journal* and two ballots over the *New York Times* and *Washington Post.* It is by far the dominant paper west of the Mississippi River.

The *Times* is definitely a major force in national and international journalism, enjoying a circulation of 1,070,000, and leading all dailies in total advertising linage and in space allocated to editorial material. Its supplementary news service—shared with the *Washington Post*—is the largest in the world, with about five hundred clients. The *Times* has seven national bureaus, twenty foreign bureaus, and five bureaus within California.

The *Los Angeles Times* has an extremely conservative heritage, somewhat like that of the *Chicago Tribune.* It was founded in 1881 and Harrison Gray Otis assumed control the following year, becoming a civic booster of unlimited energy. He also was a stalwart of the Republican party, supporting anti-union causes all of his life. The *Times* was dynamited in 1910 and his hatred of unionism intensified.

Otis' son-in-law, Harry Chandler, was equally reactionary as he fought the Hearst papers in Los Angeles for circulation. The paper's political editor, Kyle Palmer, was known to be so biased in his coverage that in 1937 Washington correspondents voted the *Los Angeles Times,* next to the Hearst and McCormick papers, as "least fair and reliable." The next publisher was Norman Chandler, much more moderate than his predecessors, but the paper lacked intensity until Norman's son Otis, then only thirty-two, assumed the publisher's chair in 1960. Within a few years the *Times* began to receive plaudits for its improved national and foreign coverage, new Sunday sections, affiliation with the *Washington Post* in the supplementary wire service, and more open-mindedness on controversial issues. (Nick Williams was editor.)

The paper also won the 1966 local coverage award for reporting the

Watts riot; the 1969 international reporting and public service awards, the latter for an exposure in city government; and in 1976 for editorial writing, 1978 for national reporting, and 1982 for music criticism. The *Times* bitterly fought the extremist Mayor Sam Yorty and joined in a coalition successfully electing his black opponent, Tom Bradley. Early in 1971 it called on President Nixon for an immediate withdrawal of troops from Vietnam. Lacking faith in George McGovern's foreign and domestic plans, and hesitant to join the *Washington Post* in declining to endorse, the *Times* supported reelection of Nixon in 1972. Embarrassed by this sad decision, the *Times* initiated a policy of not endorsing for president and other high offices. The *Times* printed numerous Watergate exposure stories, denounced Nixon in 1974, and continued to develop a tradition of strong interpretative reporting. In the early 1980s its foreign correspondents produced a number of notable stories from the Middle East and Central America.

The *Times* had moved further onto the national stage through Chandler's 1970 purchase of both *Newsday* and the *Dallas Times Herald.* Later the *Denver Post* and *Hartford Courant* were added. William F. Thomas replaced Williams as editor in 1971. A major change occurred in 1977 when Tom Johnson, the youthful publisher of the *Times Herald,* was brought to the *Times* as president and chief operating officer. Three years later he became the first nonfamily member to assume the publisher's chair, as Chandler moved into the position of editor in chief of the entire Times Mirror Corporation. Donald F. Wright then moved from the publisher's job at *Newsday* to the *Times* presidency.

The huge news staff was headed by Thomas, managing editor George Cotliar, and national editor Dennis Britton. Pulitzer Prize winner Jack Nelson ran the Washington bureau, one of the largest, and Anthony Day was in charge of the skillfully edited editorial pages. Jean Sharley Taylor was associate editor.

Despite its great talent and advertising power, the paper faced stiff competition from the *Register* in Orange County and to a lesser extent, the *Daily News,* a *Chicago Tribune*-owned paper in the San Fernando Valley, and a dozen other daily community papers with loyal readers. Within the city limits, an area serving three million of Los Angeles County's seven million persons, the *Times* ran into severe criticism for not paying appropriate attention to the blacks of South Central Los Angeles and the burgeoning Latino population, centered mainly in East Los Angeles but rapidly spreading to other areas. It was estimated that by 1990 the city's population would be heavily Latino. However, the paper's obvious advertising strength was in the affluent suburban areas where the decision was made to compete more strongly with papers serving those areas. The only metropolitan competition was the faltering *Herald-Examiner,* once a threat but reduced to a shadow of its former self.

Its forthright, thoughtful editorials—with some exceptions, particularly in the area of press freedom—seemed to lack passion, in keeping with the generally cautious attitude of the paper's management, just as the paper itself was never considered "exciting" in design or presentation. Still, the *Times* clearly had moved from a staunch Republican position into one of open-mindedness and independence. In 1982 the paper endorsed far more Democrats for office than Republicans.

The Chicago Tribune

The *Chicago Tribune* was ranked fifth in the "top 10" responses and earned enough "top 5" regional support to merit an overall fifth place position. Because the top four papers occupied those positions in nearly every region, it was difficult for any other paper to accumulate points. The *Tribune,* however, placed fifth in its own Midwest region in the "top 5" picks and was tied for third and fourth with the *Los Angeles Times* in that region's "top 10" choices.

The *Tribune's* responsiveness in recent years to social change in its own city and in the nation has earned it the respect of knowledgeable professionals. But the paper still suffers from a poor reputation dating to the days of Colonel Robert R. McCormick, the long-time publisher of the *Tribune* whose ultraconservative, isolationist views brought him severe criticism. McCormick died in 1955, but it was not until the 1970s that changes began to be apparent.

Nearly as old as Chicago itself, the paper appeared in 1847 and came under the control of Joseph Medill in 1855. Medill turned it into the city's leading daily and ran it with a firm hand until his death in 1899, at which time it was in competition with other dailies including the *Daily News.* In the twentieth century the dominant name in *Tribune* history was that of McCormick, who rivaled William Randolph Hearst when it came to reactionary politics and sensationalism from the 1920s through the early 1950s.

Yet the paper called itself "World's Greatest Newspaper" and in actuality was the "Bible of the Midwest" for many years. A distinguished foreign staff earned the paper much attention and its local coverage was strong. Key McCormick executives took over his *Tribune* in the absence of direct family heirs, and unswervingly continued its policies for more than a decade. The *Chicago American* was purchased from Hearst in 1956 and renamed *Chicago Today,* afternoon rival for the *Daily News.* Under Editor W. D. Maxwell the *Tribune* viewed the social and racial crises of the 1960s with uncompromising law-and-order stances that perpetuated the image of the doughty Colonel. As a result, its circulation lead was eroded by its morning rival, the *Sun-Times.*

Tempo
SISKEL REVIEW
'Twilight Zone—The Movie'

Tempo
BEST BURGERS
Our critic finds Chicago's top 13

Chicago Tribune
25c   Friday, June 24, 1983

Good morning

Sox, Cubs keep streaking

The Sox win their fifth game in a row, beating Minnesota 8-6. The Cubs drop their fifth in a row, losing 5-2 to Pittsburgh. In Sports.

Continental cuts loan rates

Continental Bank announces reductions in interest rate charges for many types of consumer loans, effective Friday. In Business.

Cicero plant closing reported

Western Electric Co. reportedly will close its sprawling Hawthorne Works in Cicero, which employs 4,000 people. In Business.

Arafat vows a firm grip

Meeting with Tribune correspondent Ray Moseley in Lebanon, PLO leader Yasser Arafat [right] accuses the Syrians of meddling and vows to hold power. Page 3.

Flood pours from Utah lake

Utah flooding worsens after a dam breaks, and a federal official admits that miscalculation helped cause Westlift floods. Page 3.

House tightens abortion law

The Illinois House passes legislation that would make it more difficult for a woman to have an abortion. Sec. 2, pg. 1

Pier still may be redeveloped

Mayor Harold Washington said Thursday that the future of Navy Pier will be decided within 30 days. Sec. 2, pg. 1

Weather

CHICAGO AND VICINITY: Friday: Mostly sunny; high 88 degrees, but in the 70s near the lake. Winds will be northeast at 8 to 12 miles an hour. Friday night: Fair; low 65. Saturday: Partly sunny and humid; high 90.

Court chops into congressional power

By Glen Elsasser
Chicago Tribune

WASHINGTON—In a historic decision with broad implications for the balance of powers between the presidency and Congress, the Supreme Court ruled Thursday that the legislative branch had exceeded its constitutional powers by reserving for itself an absolute "legislative veto" over executive branch decisions.

The long-awaited ruling in a deportation case immediately called into question the constitutionality of more than 200 laws that permit one or both houses of Congress to

● Under the Supreme Court ruling, a shocked Congress is left to search for new ways to control the federal bureaucracy. Page 20.

nullify decisions made elsewhere in government.

Laws containing such provisions affect a broad range of policies and agencies, among them foreign affairs, national security, defense spending, trade, energy, the Federal Trade Commission, and the Environmental Protection Agency.

What will happen to these laws is uncertain and will hinge on future actions by the court and by Congress.

The 6-2 ruling struck down a veto provision of the Immigration and Nationality Act, which gave the Senate or the House power to reverse the attorney general's decision to suspend a deportation order.

A SENATE OFFICIAL said that the im-

pact of Thursday's decision will be determined by the high court's action in two pending cases that also involve legislative vetoes. This could occur before the end of the current term this month or early next month.

One of these cases involves a two-house veto provision; the other raises the issue of whether such laws remain in effect when their veto authority is invalidated. The court said the attorney general retains authority over deportations, though the

Continued on page 20, col. 1

Congress OKs budget

State faces sanctions on dirty air

By Casey Bukro
Environment writer

IN A MAJOR policy change, federal environment chief William Ruckelshaus announced Thursday that the Environmental Protection Agency will not punish states for clean air deadline violations if they are making progress, but Illinois could be among the exceptions.

Although the move appears to weaken enforcement of the Clean Air Act, Ruckelshaus told the Air Pollution Control Association meeting in Atlanta that "It seems fundamentally

ly unfair to impose sanctions when states have made reasonable efforts to address their air quality problems" with EPA approval.

Under the act, the government could punish states that failed to meet a Dec. 31, 1982, air quality deadline by withholding billions of dollars in federal highway construction and air quality grants.

LAST FEBRUARY, the EPA named 213 counties across the nation, including Cook County and eight others in Illinois, as violators subject to punishment.

David Kee, the EPA's regional director of air management, said Illinois is considered a recalcitrant on clean air and is likely to be among those states that will not benefit from the policy change.

"Illinois is going to get sanctioned for failure to have an auto inspection-maintenance program," Kee said. "We're fairly likely to see highway grant sanctions in Cook, Kane, Du Page, and Lake Counties"

Continued on page 14, col. 1

Proudly wearing a traditional highlander's hat from Poland, President Reagan greets well-wishers during his visit to the Polish National

Tribune photo by Jerry Tomaselli
Alliance headquarters on the Northwest Side Thursday. The hat was presented to him by one of the members of the alliance.

Tax-cut cap also passes in House

By Dorothy Collin and James O'Shea
Chicago Tribune

WASHINGTON—In a defeat for President Reagan, Congress gave final legislative approval Thursday to a hotly disputed $68.3 billion budget for fiscal 1984, and the Democratic-controlled House approved a $720 limit on the third year of Reagan's tax cut.

Passage of the budget capped a long, agonizing battle and set up months of confrontation between Congress and the White House over spending and tax bills. Reagan disagrees with many details of the budget and has threatened a string of vetoes of spending and tax measures.

The $720-per-family tax-cut cap, hatched by Speaker Thomas P. O'Neill [D., Mass.], is in jeopardy despite its House passage. Many Democrats in the Senate oppose it, and Reagan has threatened to veto it. The Democratic opposition seems to ensure that a veto would not be overturned. It is expected to come up in the Senate next week.

The budget, hammered out by a House-Senate conference committee, would boost taxes by $73 billion over three years, provide at least $15 billion more in domestic spending than Reagan wants and set military spending increases at an inflation-adjusted 5 percent a year, half what the President wants.

THE BUDGET resolution does not have to be signed by the President and does not represent approval of tax and spending increases. It only sets spending targets and tax targets that Congress later will, for the most part, have to meet in considering legislation.

The House approved the budget

Continued on page 2, col. 1

Reagan lauds Poles in visit here

By Storer Rowley

BEFORE A POLISH-AMERICAN audience on the Northwest Side Thursday, President Reagan broke his silence on Pope John Paul II's pilgrimage to his native Poland and called on the Polish government to end martial law and release political prisoners.

Reagan praised the pontiff's eight-day effort to ease repression in his homeland and also reaffirmed this country's willingness to aid the Polish economy once the regime there ends its tough restrictions.

"I urge the Polish authorities to translate the restraint they showed during the papal visit into willingness to move toward reconciliation rather

● Pope John Paul II meets with Solidarity leader Lech Walesa and then returns to Rome after 8-day visit to his homeland. Page 2

than confrontation with the Polish people," Reagan told about 400 people on a brief stop outside the headquarters of the Polish National Alliance, 6100 N. Cicero Ave.

"There is only one way for the Polish government to gain the confidence and trust of its own people," Reagan said, "and that is to end martial law, to release political prisoners, to restore freely formed trade unions and to embark on a

Continued on page 19, col. 1

The chairman's revolving door

Ald. Wilson Frost [left] is followed by an aide while leaving his office as chairman of the Finance Committee Thursday. Later in the day, Ald. Edward M. Burke [right] moves into the office to

Tribune photos by Ernie Cox Jr.
assume the chairmanship, a day after the Illinois Supreme Court ruled in favor of his faction in the Chicago City Council reorganization fight. Stories in Sec. 2, pg. 1

Kennedy's personality is preserved on tapes

By Jon Margolis
Chicago Tribune

BOSTON—Angry mobs were in the streets, his state university was in disarray, and he was provoking the greatest constitutional crisis of the century. But at the end of his telephone conversation with the President of the United States, the governor of Mississippi suddenly changed the subject.

"I appreciate your interest in our poultry program and all these things," Gov. Ross Barnett said to John Kennedy, who was on the phone in the White House, probably in the Cabinet Room.

"Well," Kennedy said, "we're . . ." Then he stopped talking and, perhaps taking the phone away from his mouth, he laughed softly.

That exchange was only one of many between Kennedy and his friends, aides and adversaries that were recorded in the White House between 1962 and 1963. They were released Thursday by the John F. Kennedy Library in Boston. The 11 tape cassettes made public include 41 conversations, some over the telephone and some among top officials meeting in the Oval Office.

THE DIVERSION did Barnett little good. Neither did his subsequent pleas that Kennedy delay or abandon the court-ordered enrollment of James Meredith as the first

Kennedy   Barnett

Full coverage on Page 21.

black student at the University of Mississippi.

"This is not my order," Kennedy told him. "I just have to carry it out. So I want to get together and try to do it with you in a way which is the most satisfactory."

Barnett ignored Kennedy's appeal to use the state police to maintain order and to enroll Meredith in the university. Finally, on the last day of September, 1962, troopers and U.S. marshals escorted Meredith to the

Continued on page 21, col. 1

It was during the tenure of Clayton Kirkpatrick, who became editor in 1969, that the *Tribune's* strident editorial voice was restrained. Authority was given to younger staff members and the slogan "the American paper for Americans" was dropped. The news staff was expanded and between 1971 and 1976 the paper won three Pulitzer Prizes for local investigative reporting and foreign reporting. The *Tribune* closed *Chicago Today* in 1974, as the *Sun-Times* crept to within one-hundred-thousand in circulation.

The competition between the *Tribune* and *Sun-Times* proved fatal for the *Daily News,* also a victim of declining afternoon readership. Its 1978 demise resulted in a one hundred thousand circulation gap once more. Kirkpatrick retired and Maxwell McCrohon became president of the Chicago Tribune Company. James T. Squires, editor of the company's *Orlando Sentinel-Star,* became *Tribune* editor; Stanton R. Cook was publisher and board chairman. The company also owned an expanding *Daily News* in the San Fernando Valley area of Los Angeles, retained its ownership of the faltering *New York Daily News* after vainly trying to sell it in 1982, and bought the Chicago Cubs baseball team. In 1982 the *Tribune* opened a "state of the art" printing center that transformed the paper's appearance with lavish use of color. Daily circulation in 1983 was 760,000.

The Christian Science Monitor

The *Christian Science Monitor,* one of a handful of nationally read dailies because of its satellite delivery service, has long been established as a specialized interpretative newspaper. Respondents ranked the *Monitor* fifth in four different regions when selecting the "top 5": New England, Gulf, Southwest, and Far West. Among the "top 10" choices the paper finished sixth in New England, the Far West, and the Gulf area, and tied for sixth in the Rocky Mountain and Plains area.

The far-flung popularity ratings demonstrate the power of the satellite and the paper's thoughtful presentation of major issues.

The *Monitor* was begun in 1908 by Mary Baker Eddy, founder of the Church of Christ, Scientist, in protest against the sensationalism of other dailies and their emphasis on news of crimes and disasters. It was not intended to be, and did not become, a religious propaganda organ, but rather a serious-minded afternoon daily. Since by Christian Science tenets it avoided or minimized stories involving disasters, crime, or death, it had space in which to develop Washington and foreign correspondence, significant regional stories from around the country, and features dealing with literature, music, and art. Eventually it became noted for its

THE CHRISTIAN SCIENCE MONITOR
AN INTERNATIONAL DAILY NEWSPAPER

Soviet sculpture, United Nations Park, N.Y.   By Gordon N. Converse, chief photographer

Swords into plowshares — symbol of East German peace movement

Kremlin puts heavy thumb on dissidents and peace groups

Andropov's tactics spur conspiratorial response

By Ned Temko
Staff correspondent of
The Christian Science Monitor
Moscow

Recent arrests, trials, imprisonments, and exiles are but the dotting of "i's," the crossing of "t's".

The Soviet "dissident movement" — in the form in which this small band of writers, scientists, artists, and political thinkers came to be known in the 1960s and '70s — is finished.

"Liquidated," pronounces one of its few, now nearly silent, survivors with a resigned sort of sorrow. He recalls aloud the increasingly sophisticated mix of arrests, trials, and expulsions whereby the powers that be have picked off the major dissident figures one by one.

"Forgotten" by the world and news media outside, says another one, more bitterly.

Among the figures who share this lament is Yelena Bonner, wife of Nobel Prize-winner Andrei

Sakharov. Exiled without trial for his "anti-Soviet" stance on human rights, the man who was once the establishment's foremost nuclear physicist has lived since early 1980 in the Russian city of Gorky, which is closed to foreigners.

And the era of large-scale Jewish emigration also seems over, at least for the foreseeable future. One dotted "i," for Jews who want to leave, was the unveiling of a Soviet "Anti-Zionist Committee" at a news conference earlier this month.

Still, dissent of a kind seems likely to go on. The pattern of Russian history and the odd genius of the Soviet system for alienating even the gentler of its critics would appear to guarantee this. Another guarantee may derive partly from the years of superpower detente. Soviet society as a whole is irresolutely, if not overwhelmingly, more open to foreign influence than in decades past.

But with the major dissidents of the 1960s and '70s all silenced or isolated, Soviet dissent, at least

★ Please turn to Page 12

East bloc tries to keep its doves in tight cages

By David Fouquet
Special to The Christian Science Monitor
Brussels

Roland Jahn arrived in West Germany by train last week, deprived of his East German citizenship — the latest example of the seriousness with which communist officials view the growing peace movements within the East bloc.

Mr. Jahn was the 20th member of the peace movement in the East German town of Jena to be so expelled to the West. He said he had been pressured into applying for a visa to leave East Germany and forced onto a train by security forces.

Once scorned by Western officials and activists as mere propaganda appendages of their manipulative governments, some communist-bloc peace and antinuclear protesters now are seen as an increasingly independent force. And they are beginning to attract public support.

In recent weeks, a West European government has prepared an internal document detailing this growing phenomenon in the Soviet bloc. A leading Western peace and disarmament publication has given it wide coverage. And last month a number of prominent members of the West German Green Party demonstrated on Alexanderplatz, East Berlin's main square, before they were detained and ousted by the police there.

Western contacts and attitudes toward the official and unofficial movements in the East have sometimes been ambiguous. Some Western protest groups and activists want nothing to do with the official communist peace organs, such as the Moscow-sponsored World Peace Council, which is holding "a world assembly for peace and life against nuclear war" June 21 to 26 in Prague. Most Western activists prefer to deal with the

★ Please turn to Page 12

Impact of Pentagon efforts to tighten its spending practices

By Brad Knickerbocker
Staff correspondent of The Christian Science Monitor
Washington

Congress this week takes up the Reagan administration's $188 billion military procurement bill for 1984. Included are such controversial items as the MX strategic nuclear missile and chemical weapons.

Lawmakers aren't expected to make massive changes in the Pentagon's list of desired weaponry. Instead, they are more likely to snip around the edges so that the final tab represents 5 to 6 percent real growth, instead of the 10 percent requested by the President.

The more vital debate may be over how the Defense Department spends money and the likely impact of that spending on the United States economy. The Pentagon's procurement procedures have a direct bearing on the final cost of a weapon system. Defense purchases account for more than two-thirds of all federal buying. That portion will continue to increase: Total defense spending for the eight potential Reagan years is projected to be about $2 trillion, so the economic results could be significant.

Defense Secretary Caspar W. Weinberger told a National Press Club audience Tuesday that the Pentagon expects to save significant amounts of money by using more

efficient and economical procurement procedures. Secretary Weinberger cited multimillion-dollar savings from a new crackdown on corruption, from tightening up defense contracting, and from such management reforms as multiyear procurement and more competition.

He called these "a campaign as important to our national security as any military campaign." On the same day, Deputy Defense Secretary Paul Thayer announced a "new emphasis" on initiatives to improve defense acquisition that were begun two years ago by his predecessor.

Weinberger sees significant savings   By a staff photographer

Frank Carlucci. On Monday, Mr. Carlucci, now president of Sears World Trade Inc., said Congress was responsible for some $20 billion in higher military procurement costs because of faulty budgeting. "The key to efficient procurement is budget stability," he said in a speech at the Brookings Institution.

Pentagon budgeteers say program and management initiatives reflected in the 1984 budget should save taxpayers nearly $50 billion through 1988.

But according to a recent report by the General Accounting Office, such claimed savings for the current fiscal year may have been overstated. It said significant portions were questionable or not likely to be realized. This adds to doubts about future savings.

The Pentagon's case is not helped by such things as the recent Air Force acknowledgment that the cost of a single ground-launched cruise missile jumped $500,000 in the past 18 months, and that total program costs have doubled during the past five years. The Air Force says this is largely because of a congressional reduction in the number of missiles to be purchased, which raises the unit cost.

The projected economic impact of increased defense buying on the nation's economy is also hotly debated.

★ Please turn to Page 18

ability to sit back periodically and take a long-view look at major news developments.

In its first ten years the *Monitor* gained 120,000 readers under the editorship of Frederick Dixon, then was temporarily disrupted by a dispute over its management. Editor Willis J. Abbot helped to restore its prestige in the 1920s. But the *Monitor's* outstanding editor was Erwin D. Canham, who joined the staff in 1925 and served as a Washington and foreign correspondent before becoming managing editor in 1940 and editor in 1945. Canham's voice was often raised in discussions of journalistic problems and his professional associates soon came to regard him as an influential editor of a great newspaper.

In 1964 Canham went into semiretirement and DeWitt John, a former *Monitor* foreign correspondent, was named editor to help reverse a circulation slump that had touched 185,000. The *Monitor* adopted a five-column front-page makeup, larger type, splashy art work, and more sparkling writing. Before 1970 the staff had won two national reporting Pulitzer Prizes and an international award. During the next decade the *Monitor's* quality improved, but circulation fluctuated from 260,000 to 180,000. Earl W. Froell was editor and Charlotte Saikowski edited a superior editorial page. Godfrey Sperling headed Washington coverage, long famed for the reporting of Richard L. Strout. Published in Boston, the *Monitor* also printed regional editions in New Jersey, Chicago, and Los Angeles, and an international edition in London. Circulation was approximately 150,000.

The Philadelphia Inquirer

Making a strong pitch for national attention in the survey was the *Philadelphia Inquirer,* a Knight-Ridder newspaper that has been earning a reputation for "project journalism." The *Inquirer* placed fifth among the "top 5" choices in its Eastern region and in the area from Montana to Kansas, and tied for fifth and sixth in the Mid-Atlantic area. It received ten votes for first place in the overall "top 5" competition, more than the *Chicago Tribune.*

Competing for attention in the Knight-Ridder newspaper group in the past decade, as a rival to the *Miami Herald* and *Detroit Free Press,* the *Inquirer* was described before its 1970 purchase by John S. Knight as an "unqualifiedly awful paper." Knight brought Eugene L. Roberts, Jr., forty-year-old national editor of the *New York Times,* to Philadelphia and gave him free rein as executive editor to compete with the *Bulletin,* long advertised as the paper nearly everybody read. Beginning in 1975 the *Inquirer* staff, under Roberts' prodding, won six consecutive Pulitzer

Bingo! 'How to live to be 100 — or more'

In TV Week: New Bingo game cards. In Family/Home/Fashion: The first of three excerpts from George Burns' new book.

The Philadelphia Inquirer

Vol. 308, No. 170　　　©1983, Philadelphia Newspapers Inc.　　　Sunday, June 19, 1983　　　ONE DOLLAR

Life, death and hope: How science tussles with AIDS

By Donald C. Drake
Inquirer Staff Writer

A mystery in the blood
Another in an occasional series.

BETHESDA, Md. — Dr. H. Clifford Lane, a research immunologist at the National Institutes of Health, rushed up the stairs of the clinical center and headed toward the office of his boss, Dr. Anthony S. Fauci.

(See AIDS on 10-A)

Shuttle is up; sexism down

1st U.S. woman in space

By Mike Leary
Inquirer Staff Writer

CAPE CANAVERAL, Fla. — Sally K. Ride, a tennis star turned astronaut, was blasted into orbit and history yesterday morning aboard the shuttle Challenger — becoming the first American woman ever to soar through space.

(See SHUTTLE on 13-A)

Gloria Steinem watches Challenger — and Sally Ride — lift off

Camden students' spirits soar as their project goes into orbit

By John Hilferty
Inquirer Staff Writer

(See ANTS on 13-A)

Volcker kept by Reagan as Fed chief

Business expected to hail decision

By Sally Jacobsen
Associated Press

WASHINGTON — President Reagan ended months of speculation yesterday by announcing he will nominate Paul A. Volcker to serve another four years as chairman of the Federal Reserve Board when his first term expires in August.

(See VOLCKER on 6-A)

Paul A. Volcker
Renomination was in question

Dioxin site found near a N.J. school

By Bob Drogin
Inquirer Staff Writer

CLIFTON, N.J. — High levels of dioxin have been confirmed in the soil at an active chemical plant located near an elementary school and dozens of homes here.

(See DIOXIN on 9-A)

A top-secret formula led to a long chase

By L. Stuart Ditzen
Inquirer Staff Writer

George Simmons, through meticulous work and incredible luck, had been amazed to learn the identity of the man he had been hunting — the man he suspected of being the Rohm & Haas spy.

(See FORMULA on 12-A)

Weather & Index

HAZY, WARM and humid today with a chance of a shower. High near 85; low, mid-60s. Full weather, Page 13-E.

SECTIONS		FEATURES	
News	A,B	Action Line	5-K
Review/Opinion	C	Bridge	4-I
Sports	D	Crossword	13-F
Business	E	Editorials	6-C
Entertainment	G	Horoscope	2-K
Travel	H	Ann Landers	2-K
Food	I	Obituaries	11-E
Family/Fashion	K	Puzzles	13-E
Real Estate	L	CLASSIFIED	
Books/Leisure	P	Index	13-E
Inquirer magazine	Astro		1-F
TV Week		Help Wanted	1-M
Comic Section		Schools	5-C

One million at shrine roar approval as Pope thanks Poles for 'solidarity'

From Inquirer Wire Services

CZESTOCHOWA, Poland — Pope John Paul II yesterday took his pilgrimage to the holiest shrine of Poland and, in a sermon to a crowd estimated at one million, used the word solidarity for the first time since his journey began.

John Paul II
Words of support cheer countrymen

(See POPE on 10-A)

prizes. One was the 1978 gold medal for reporting on police abuse in the city, another pair for national and international reporting, and two for local reporting, including the 1980 story of the Three Mile Island crisis. Cartoonist Tony Auth won in 1976.

When the *Bulletin,* faced with mounting deficits, suspended publication in 1982, Roberts persuaded the Knight-Ridder management to give him eighty new reporters and editors, five overseas news bureaus, ten new national and foreign correspondents, a new Sunday book-review section, a 20 percent larger news hole, the UPI news wire, five more photographers, and thirteen new comic strips. Before the end of the year, daily circulation had increased 30 percent and the Sunday paper became the fifth largest in the country. Principal competition was the *Inquirer's* sister paper, the afternoon *Daily News.* Roberts, known as "the Frog" to his staff and competitors, had made his soft-spoken southern presence known on the national scene, along with his paper. Daily circulation was 550,000.

The Boston Globe

Sharing attention in New England with the *Christian Science Monitor*—and claiming the distinction of offering the area's best coverage—is the *Boston Globe.* While the paper did not place high in the "top 5" competition, its total of "top 10" picks gave it enough strength to be ranked along with the two Knight-Ridder papers in positions seven, eight, and nine.

In the "top 10" responses the paper finished third in New England, fifth in the East, sixth in the Southwest, and seventh in the Deep South, Gulf area, and Far West.

The *Globe* came into contention for top national ranking in the 1970s. It was founded in 1872 and published by four generations of the Taylor family since 1873. The morning and evening *Globes,* dominating Boston newspapering since the 1960s, won national attention by joining the *New York Times* and the *Washington Post* in publishing the Pentagon Papers until stopped by court order. Under publisher Davis Taylor and editor Thomas Winship, the *Globe* in May 1967 had become the second major U.S. paper to oppose the Vietnam War, and had editorialized against the Nixon presidential candidacies in 1968 and 1972. In October 1973 it became the first major daily to call for his impeachment.

Such a record gave the *Globe* liberal credentials, which it furthered through the reporting of Washington bureau chief Martin Nolan, the cartoons of Paul Szep, and the winning of the 1975 Pulitzer gold medal for its coverage of the Boston school controversy and antibusing riots. In

Red Sox take a drubbing from the Tigers, 10-2

(In Sports Plus, the Jock Doctor — Page 39)

The Boston Globe

A good mistery
FRIDAY — Fog lifting, cloudy, 70s
SATURDAY — Some clouds, may shower
HIGH TIDE — 4:58 a.m., 5:40 p.m.
FULL REPORT — PAGE 60

Vol. 223, No. 168© 1983, Globe Newspaper Co. * * * FRIDAY, JUNE 17, 1983 Telephone 929-2000 Classified Circulation 929-1500 929-2222 76 Pages – 25 Cents

Senate votes itself a 15% raise

By David Rogers
Globe Staff

WASHINGTON – The Senate yesterday narrowly approved a 15 percent pay raise next month for members while postponing a previously adopted cap on honorariums and outside income until next January.

The 49-47 vote would bring senators' salaries up to the House level of $69,800, but the six-month delay of any cap on outside income allows members to continue to supplement their pay this year with unlimited honorariums for outside speaking engagements.

The pay amendment was attached to a $16.1-billion supplementary appropriations bill adopted moments later on a 64-33 vote. The legislation goes to a conference with the House next week.

Elsewhere in Congress, there were these developments yesterday:

– The Senate, under pressure from the banking industry, voted, 86-4, last night to approve legislation to kill tax withholding on income and dividend income scheduled to take effect next month. The bill must go to conference with the House, but anticipating approval of repeal, Treasury Secretary Donald Regan announced a 30-day postponement of the July 1 effective date, and the White House signaled a willingness to accept the version supported by Senate Finance Committee chairman Robert Dole (R-Kan.). [Page 9.]

– The Democratic-controlled House Ways and Means Committee approved a leadership-backed bill imposing a $700 cap on the final 10 percent income tax cut due July 1. Despite the endorsement of Speaker Thomas P. O'Neill Jr., four Democrats joined 11 Republicans in opposing the measure. Thus the 18-15 vote was a harbinger of the

PAY, Page 9

Pope reaches out to Poles

Pontiff, at beginning of visit, says he stands with 'all my compatriots'

By Steven Erlanger
Globe Staff

WARSAW – Pope John Paul II, on the first day of his return to an altered and expectant homeland, made clear yesterday that his thoughts were centered on those here who suffer, who are imprisoned, who are despondent, who are afraid.

In his first homily, last night, to a crowded and colorful St. John's Cathedral, the Pope declared to building applause:

"Together with all my compatriots – especially with those who are most acutely tasting the bitterness of disappointment, humiliation, suffering, of being deprived of their freedom, of being wronged, of having their dignity trampled upon – I stand beneath the Cross of Christ. . . ."

It was an elegant, moving sermon to the memory of the late Stefan Cardinal Wyszynski, John Paul's mentor, who had been imprisoned in the 1950s by the Communist government here and who is buried in St. John's. The Pope quoted from Cardinal Wyszinski's "Notes from Prison" and drew sharp parallels between his suffering and consequent strength and that of the nation. "In his giving without reserve," the Pope said, Cardinal Wyszynski "found his own spiritual freedom: Yes, he was a free man, and he taught his compatriots true freedom."

And then the Pope spoke most explicitly about the martial-law crackdown declared in December 1981, again producing sharp intakes of breath in the cathedral and strong, prolonged applause: "Divine providence spared [Cardinal Wyszynski] the sad events associated with the date of 13 December 1981."

It was a clear indication that in his own direct and yet subtle fashion, the Polish Pope on this visit would hardly ignore the pain of the nation, and would attempt to provide both balm and inspiration to the troubled, weary souls of his compatriots.

Hundreds of thousands of Poles turned out to press along the barriers that lined the Pope's motorcade from the airport to the heart of Warsaw in the Old Town. They came from Warsaw and from hundreds of miles away, gathering hours before the Pope arrived to chat and pray, sing hymns and folk songs along streets lined with banners and flags, paved with thousands of flowers arranged in national and religious symbols, like embroidery on the cobblestones.

POPE, Page 10

Pope John Paul II is flanked by Jozef Cardinal Glemp, Roman Catholic primate of Poland, and Henryk Jablonski, chairman of Poland's state council and titular head of state, as he walks across tarmac at Warsaw Okiecie International Airport on his arrival in Polish capital yesterday to begin eight-day visit to his homeland – his second since becoming Pope. At right, Lech Walesa, former leader of outlawed Solidarity labor union, watches television coverage of pontiff's arrival. With him in their Gdansk apartment are his wife and one of their children. AP, UPI PHOTOS

IN THIS CORNER

Dragonfly clutching mosquito is magnified 10 times through microscope at the Don Santo Corp. in Wellesley. GLOBE PHOTO BY STAN GROSSFELD

The dragon as mosquito-slayer

By Peter Anderson
Globe Staff

WELLS, Maine – There is this question: How many mosquitos can a hungry dragonfly eat if a hungry dragonfly eats mosquitos all day long? That is not a riddle but a matter of public interest here. One Maine entomologist estimates each dragonfly probably eats 100 mosquitos a day. Thus the 14,000 dragonflies the town of Wells imported from Massachusetts could be devouring 1.4 million mosquitos a day, 42 million mosquitos a month.

A lot of people in this part of south coastal Maine think the dragonflies work and pay $10 for 50 of them. Wells motel owner Robert Zalko says fogging

IN THIS CORNER, Page 11

Panel: Apology, $20,000 due WWII internees

By Mike Feinsilber
Associated Press

WASHINGTON – A commission recommended yesterday that the federal government apologize to the people of Japanese ancestry who were put in isolated camps during World War II and pay $20,000 to each of approximately 60,000 internees still living.

The recommendation to spend $1.5 billion in compensation and other forms of redress for the detention was sent to Congress after a two-year investigation by the Commission on Wartime Relocation and Internment of Civilians. The commission declared no justification for the episode existed and blamed it on war hysteria, racial hatred and a failure of political leadership.

No congressional action is expected for several years, and even then it remains in doubt that Congress will accept the commission's recommendations, said Ronald K. Ikejiri, Washington representative of the Japanese American Citizens League. He expressed gratitude for the recommendation, however.

In all, 120,000 people of Japanese descent were put in detention camps under an order signed by President Franklin D. Roosevelt 10 weeks after the devastating Japanese attack on Pearl Harbor on Dec. 7, 1941. The internees included nisei, the American-born children of Japanese immigrants, as well as issei, or Japanese-born immigrants who were naturalized US citizens.

About half of them have since died and the panel did not recommend payment to their heirs.

The commission told Congress, "No amount of money can fully compensate the excluded people for their losses and sufferings.

"Two and a half years behind the barbed wire of a relocation camp, branded potentially disloyal because of one's ethnicity alone – these injustices cannot neatly be translated into dollars and cents."

INTERNMENT, Page 8

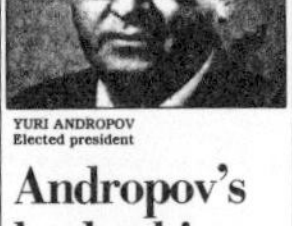

YURI ANDROPOV
Elected president

Andropov's leadership reaffirmed

By Dusko Doder
Washington Post

MOSCOW – Yuri Andropov, the Soviet Communist Party leader, was elected president yesterday in a move reaffirming his dominant position in the Kremlin leadership.

The two chambers of the Supreme Soviet, meeting in joint session at the Kremlin, made the decision unanimously. The action capped a swift consolidation of power and authority by the former KGB chief who succeeded the late Leonid Brezhnev as general secretary of the Communist Party seven months ago.

As general secretary and chief of the Defense Council, or commander in chief of the armed forces, Andropov already held the two most powerful positions in the country. The presidency, a largely ceremonial post, gives him added prestige, authority and flexibility, particularly in foreign affairs.

After the vote by the 1500 deputies, Andropov made a short acceptance speech, after which he rose to acknowledge a standing ovation. A microphone placed at his seat, perhaps because of his apparent

SOVIETS, Page 8

Housing starts, factory use in US hit peaks in May

By Pauline Jelinek
Associated Press

WASHINGTON – Housing starts hit a 3½-year peak and the nation's factories operated at the highest level in 15 months last month as the recovery spread throughout American industry, government figures indicated yesterday.

The news added fuel to a stock market rally, with the Dow Jones average of 30 industrial stocks surging 11.02 points to 1248.30 – adding to the record set Wednesday. Page 32.

Separately, the government said its broadest measure of US foreign trade showed a $3.05 billion deficit in the first quarter of the year, down from $6.6 billion in the final three months of 1982.

Officials at the Commerce Department, which compiled the foreign trade report, have said they expect the deficit to widen to $20 billion for 1983. They say this is because the slower pace of the rebound abroad will mean slower growth in US exports than in imports, and the strong dollar will make American goods more expensive to US trading partners.

About $94 million in low-interest mortgages will be made available to 2000 Massachusetts residents in early August, using a voucher system, state officials announced yesterday. Page 4.

In a brighter showing for the construction industry, Commerce reported that work on new housing was started at an annual rate of 1.79 million units last month, a climb of 19.1 percent from April.

The increase followed declines of 10 percent and 6.3 percent the two previous months and put housing starts at their highest level since the 1.8 million units of September 1979, the report said.

The report also said building permits for future construction rose 5.6 percent to

ECONOMY, Page 4

1-year sentence for cruelty to cats

By Wendy Fox
Globe Staff

A lot of people are cruel to animals and never get caught, but Hull animal control officer Vicki Smythe says Norman B. Day's case was pretty clear-cut.

This week in Hingham District Court, Day, 24, of Nantucket, received two consecutive six-month sentences for throwing two kittens from a porch in Hull last month. One kitten landed onto a street crowded with traffic and the other onto a sidewalk. Two Hull policemen said they saw him do it.

Judge Alvin C. Tamkin found Day guilty of disorderly conduct and cruelty. He sentenced him to serve the terms in the Plymouth County House of Correction and fined him $1375. Day, who didn't deny hurling the 6-week-old kittens, said he'll appeal the case in the hope of overturning or at least reducing his sentence. He was released on personal recognizance pending his appeal.

"I thought it was terribly cruel," Tamkin said yesterday. "I understand he just tossed them out." Day could not be reached for comment.

Hull Police Sgt. Robert Jeffrey told the judge in court Wednesday that on May 8, two patrolmen saw Day throw the kittens 50 feet from the porch at 658 Nantasket av. Jeffrey said Day told the officers one kitten had scratched his leg as he sat on the porch.

Smythe said yesterday that police called her as soon as they plucked the kittens from the street, and she took them to a veterinarian. One of the kittens had a broken nose, she said, and the other was just shaken.

CATS, Page 11

1980 the paper was awarded a nearly unprecedented three Pulitzer prizes when its local reporting group called the Spotlight Team, columnist Ellen Goodman, and critic William A. Henry III all won. In 1983 the *Globe* scored once more.

General Charles H. Taylor took over the *Globe* as publisher in 1873 and editor after 1880, making it a sensationalized New Journalism product catching the eye of Joseph Pulitzer. The first William O. Taylor held both posts until 1955, when Davis Taylor became publisher and Laurence Winship, managing editor since 1937, took over as editor. Thomas Winship, his son, became editor in 1965 and was instrumental in giving the *Globe* its "new look." Winning national attention, he was elected ASNE president in 1980. The second William O. Taylor became publisher in 1978. The two *Globes* were merged into an all-day publication in 1979. The daily circulation was 510,000.

The Miami Herald

The leading paper in the South is the *Miami Herald*. Survey results showed it finishing fifth in the "top 10" choices in the Deep South and Mid-Atlantic states, sixth in the East and Midwest, tied for sixth in the Rocky Mountain-Plains region, eighth in the Far West—all evidence of strong national strength. Miami placed fifth in its region in the "top 5" responses and was first in its regional competition, ahead of the *St. Petersburg Times* and *Atlanta Constitution*.

The *Miami Herald* had won its way to national recognition by 1970 as a member of the Knight-Ridder newspaper group. John S. Knight began his career in the 1920s on the family's *Akron Beacon-Journal*. Their first expansion outside Ohio was to the *Miami Herald* in 1937. Purchase of the *Detroit Free Press* in 1940 gave the Knights a major group, to which they added the Charlotte and Macon newspapers and the *Philadelphia Inquirer* and *Daily News*. James L. Knight, a brother, concentrated his interest on the Miami and Charlotte operations, while John Knight focused on Detroit. But the management was integrated. In 1974 the Knights merged their sixteen-daily group with Ridder Publications, which owned or had a substantial interest in nineteen dailies. The new Knight-Ridder had the largest combined circulation of all U.S. groups. Added were such major Ridder papers as the *St. Paul Dispatch* and *Pioneer Press* and the *San Jose Mercury and News*.

Lee Hills joined the *Miami Herald* in 1942, coming from the Scripps-Howard papers. As managing editor, he built up the Latin American coverage of the *Herald* and began an international air express edition.

John S. Knight had written his famed column, "The Editor's

Are Florida ad agencies major league? Business / Monday

Partly
Cloudy
Details on 2A

The Miami Herald

First
Edition

100 pages   Monday, June 20, 1983   25 cents

Pope: 'We cannot be slaves'

**Polish regime warns that protests
could prolong martial law restrictions.**

From Herald Wire Services

CZESTOCHOWA, Poland —
Pope John Paul II celebrated Sunday mass before more than a million people at the home of Poland's holiest Catholic shrine and sternly lectured the Communist regime that freedom "is given to man by God."

In an implicit rebuke to Poland's military regime, the pope said the state is firmly sovereign only "when it governs society and also serves the common good of society and allows the nation to realize its own subjectivity, its own identity.

"The sovignty of the state is

deeply linked to its capacity to promote the freedom of the nation, that is, to developing conditions that permit the nation to express all of its distinctive historical and cultural identity . . ."

"As children of God, we cannot be slaves," John Paul said.

Many in the throng raised their fingers in the V-for-victory sign of the banned Solidarity labor movement and sang the patriotic hymn *God Who Watches Over Poland.* Solidarity banners were raised above the sea of rapt faces at the end of the two-hour service.

Large anti-government demonstrations marked the pontiff's first three nights in his homeland, including a march by 50,000 people past the Warsaw Communist Party headquarters that was the biggest protest since martial law was declared Dec. 13, 1981.

Those outpourings of emotion, perhaps prompted in part by the pope's repeated criticism of the Communist regime, brought a warning from the government. Spokesman Jerzy Urban said on Sunday that continued demonstrations could delay the end of martial law, which was partially lifted in December after a year in force.

Urban also hinted that the church was not keeping its part of the bar-

gain for the papal visit. He said the authorities "expect the church side to adhere to the religious aspect of the visit" to this devoutly Roman Catholic nation.

John Paul has attempted to keep the emotional outbursts of Polish Catholics in check to avoid touching off political unrest.

Yet the pope declared Sunday, "Freedom is given to man by God."

Despite a cold drizzle, more than a million people packed the gentle slopes around the Jasna Gora monastery for the open-air mass, which honored the 600th anniversary of the presence in the monastery of the ancient "black madonna" icon

Please turn to POPE / 8A   Pope greets people from southern Poland's mountain region.

Doctors' fast grows in Israel

**1,000 take part
in hunger strike**

From Herald Wire Services

TEL AVIV — A hunger protest among Israel's public-health physicians had grown Sunday to include 1,000 doctors in all 17 major hospitals in the latest tactic in a 2½-month-old dispute with the government over pay and work hours.

At Soroka Hospital in the Negev Desert city of Beersheba — where doctors began their fast on Tuesday — two of three surgical wards had been emptied and patients sent home. Some doctors were reported unable to work as a result of the fast. Soroka's director, David Ronen, said the facility's emergency cases were being flown to Jerusalem hospitals.

Some patients at the Negev hospital said they were joining the fast in solidarity with the physicians; others lashed out at the strikers.

"You are hurting us! You are hurting our children!" shouted one parent whose child was turned away from the emergency room.

"We will stop fasting immediately — the minute our struggle is taken out of [Finance Minister Yoram] Aridor's hands," said Dr. David Pest, a senior urologist at Soroka.

"We have come to the conclusion that the only thing left for us to do is to hurt ourselves," Pest said in a telephone interview. He said four hunger strikers collapsed Sunday.

Asked whether patients might die because of the hunger strike, a Soroka surgeon, Dr. Ivor Sover, told the Armed Forces Radio that the future of "medical services in this country is worth more than the life of one person or another."

Doctors began fasting in other hospitals Saturday and Sunday.

The Cabinet discussed the crisis at its regular Sunday meeting. Newspapers reported that a plan was being considered to replace the hunger strikers with army doctors, but a Cabinet spokesman denied it.

Spokesman Dan Meridor said that Prime Minister Menachem Begin promised to summon Aridor and Health Minister Eliezer Shostak, and a senior official said they would meet today. He added, however, that Begin's sole aim was to end a dispute between Aridor and Shostak over how to deal with the 8,500 doctors and their 78-day-old wage dispute. The official, who declined to be identified, said Begin would not make any new offer to the doctors.

The doctors say that they gross the equivalent of $600 to $1,120 a month. They want salaries of $925 a month for a 36-hour work week instead of the 45 hours they work now.

They contend that the only solu-

Please turn to DOCTORS / 8A

A lad and his dad

Gee, dad, we should do this every day, Matthew Moody, 5, seems to be saying to his father, Tim. Many mothers got a day of rest Sunday as children and dads built Father's Day memories. The weather in Coconut Grove was particularly good for sharing outdoor fun.

Second Satellite Parked in Space

Challenger completes major goals

By MIKE TONER
Herald Science Writer

HOUSTON — The space shuttle Challenger's five-member crew chalked up its second major delivery Sunday as Sally Ride, the first American woman in space, sent a $20-million Indonesian communications satellite spinning off on its way to a permanent parking place in space.

Ride reported that the 2,500-pound satellite jarred the shuttle with "a good kick" as it popped free of its restraining latches and floated out of the shuttle's cargo hold 185 miles over the Atlantic Ocean.

'We are winning the war' against the rebels, says El Salvador's President Alvaro Magana.

Salvadoran 'sure' GIs won't be needed

From Herald Wire Services

WASHINGTON — President Alvaro Magaña of El Salvador said Sunday his government's security forces are winning the war against leftist guerrillas and he is "positively sure" American troops will never be needed to ensure victory.

"I'm sure that we are winning the war and for sure they [the rebels] are losing the war," Magaña said on the CBS-TV interview program "Face the Na-

tion."

Magaña's interview was recorded Saturday, shortly before he ended a two-day Washington visit in which he conferred with President Reagan and congressional leaders.

Magaña, who has served as provisional president for the past 13 months, was emphatic when asked whether American troops will be needed to defeat the

Please turn to MAGANA / 16A

Chileans lost prosperity, and now, they've lost fear

By JAMES BROOKE
Herald Staff Writer

News Analysis

SANTIAGO, Chile — Chileans have lost their fear.

That phrase was heard again and again here during the past week of protest, strikes and riots.

It came from unemployed men burning barricades in slums, angry housewives blowing car horns in middle-class neighborhoods and conservative politicians conspiring in downtown skyscrapers.

President Augusto Pinochet came to power in a bloody 1973 military coup against President Salvador Allende and has since ruled with a successful mix of political repression and economic prosperity.

But last year, Chile's "economic miracle" vanished and the country nose-dived into a serious depression. The gross national product fell by 14 per cent and unemployment and underemployment climbed to 30 per cent.

Sporadic protests grew until May 11, when Chileans turned out for

the first major protest against the military regime in 10 years. Pinochet responded with repression: 2,000 were detained and hundreds more were arrested. But the heavy-handed tactics failed to scare the protesters.

"On May 11, Chileans lost their fear," Rodolfo Seguel, head of the copper miners' union and orchestrator of the May demonstrations, said in an interview hours before he led the nation out on a second protest against the regime last Tuesday.

Seguel skillfully expanded his list of demands from narrow labor issues to a call for a return to democracy, and Chileans protested massively.

Despite Seguel's pleas for nonviolence, the protests left five dead, 70 injured, 62 police cars damaged, 100

Please turn to CHILE / 16A

Today's Chuckle

Economists seem to agree the best time to buy just about anything is last year.

Jazz greats like Al Hirt are fleeing Bourbon Street's crime and 'filth.'

Quarter's decline has New Orleans singing the blues

By BILL ROSE
Herald Staff Writer

NEW ORLEANS — Jazz trumpeter Al Hirt glowered with Falstaffian fury as a disheveled, drunken, obviously beaten young man staggered past his French Quarter doorstep with blood streaming down his face and bright red bruises covering his bare back.

"See there?" Hirt bellowed. "It goes on all the time down here. People come out of that joint over there with shivs still sticking in their belly. That's why I'm getting the hell out. None of the local people want to come down here anymore unless they have armed guards. It's filthy."

After 30 years of wowing crowds at his French Quarter nightclub with a powerful trumpet and bawdy comic patter, the portly

"pied piper of Bourbon Street" is pulling out.

He is tired of dwindling audiences, "filthy streets," nighttime stabbings, drunks asleep on his doorstep, whores who pick pockets and aggressive transvestites who teasingly call him "Miss Hirt," taunt him with pleas for sex and steal his gold cuff links.

But last week, Hirt began to extract his revenge. His abrupt departure, coming out on the heels of exits by jazz artists Pete Fountain and Woody Herman, has left New Orleans' street of jazz, sex and sizzle virtually bereft of big-name entertainers. And, coming less than a year before the 1984 World's Fair, which local officials hope will rescue a lagging tourist industry, Bourbon's steady downhill slide is forcing an agonized reappraisal of the sensuously seamy image the Crescent City has slyly

constructed over the years.

It isn't that New Orleans isn't trying. It has beefed up police patrols in the dark, narrow streets of the historic quarter. It has passed laws to halt the invasion of dozens of souvenir T-shirt shops that many feel spoils the ancient aura of the old red-light district. And, in three months, vehicles on Bourbon will be forbidden. It will become a permanent pedestrian mall with new trees, flowers and sidewalk cafes.

Crime in the quarter was down 12 per cent in the first three months of this year and, as police Capt. Dan McMullen puts it, "only 38" tourists were victims of French Quarter crime from January through April — an average of

Please turn to BOURBON / 12A

Al Hirt: Tired of dwindling audiences.

Notebook," for thirty-two years before he won the Pulitzer Prize for editorial writing in 1968. Both he and Hills served as president of the American Society of Newspaper Editors, Knight twice. Knight helped found and was president of the Inter American Press Association, which Hills later headed. Among American publishers of the 1970s, Knight was one of the most outspoken. Against participation in the Indochina war since 1954, he had a loud and clear position on that issue. Knight and his group of papers generally supported Republicans for the presidency, but deserted Senator Goldwater in 1964.

Hills stepped down as Knight-Ridder board chairman in 1979, but remained as editorial chairman. Bernard H. Ridder, Jr. succeeded him. Knight died in 1981. The same year, Shirley Christian gave his *Herald* another Pulitzer Prize, for international reporting from Central America. The *Herald* published a Spanish language edition circulating to thirty-one countries. Daily circulation was four hundred thousand.

METRO EDITION
Louisville, Ky., Tuesday morning, June 21, 1983
25¢
32 Pages
Vol. 256, No. 172
****

The Courier-Journal

Budget resolution would raise taxes, cut defense funds

From Washington Post, New York Times and AP Dispatches

WASHINGTON — House and Senate negotiators struck a deal yesterday on a 1984 budget resolution that calls for $12 billion in higher taxes, less spending for defense and a multibillion dollar standby fund for programs to ease the effects of recession.

The compromise between House- and Senate-passed versions of the budget must now be voted on by both chambers, but it has the backing of most Democratic leaders and Senate Republicans.

They believe it strikes a fair balance between the priorities of the two chambers, and holds out the only hope for maintaining some control over congressional spending.

However, the measure only sets spending ceilings and revenue floors for Congress; a budget resolution doesn't actually appropriate money to be spent on programs.

The resolution also isn't subject to a presidential veto — so Reagan has less leverage over the budget deliberations than he usually does over legislation.

However, the president has said that, regardless of the targets Congress sets, he will veto any spending and tax bills of which he doesn't approve.

Last night, White House spokesman Larry Speakes said the compromise "doesn't show a lot of prospect."

Senate Budget Committee Chairman Pete V. Domenici, R-N.M., argued that the spending and revenue totals in the compromise aren't significantly different from those proposed by the president in his January budget message.

The main difference is that Congress has added more to domestic programs, while cutting back on Reagan's military requests.

"It probably boils down to priorities," Domenici said.

The compromise was struck after almost two weeks of intensive negotiations and extensive pulse-taking in both houses.

It features three main elements:

✔ Tax increases of $73 billion over the next three years, including $12 billion in fiscal 1984, which begins on Oct. 1, $15 billion in 1985 and $46 billion in 1986.

By law, budget resolutions have to look forward three years.

The tax increases for '84 and '85 are considerably higher than the nominal increases sought by Reagan in the budget plan he submitted to Congress in January.

But the increases are in line with the $50 billion in standby tax increases Reagan wanted for 1986. The standby increases would "kick in" if deficits continued to soar.

However, Speakes said last night that "the president ... won't go for new taxes."

✔ An increase in the growth of defense spending of about 5 percent, after taking inflation into account.

This is half of what Reagan wanted, although the proposed spending-authority level of $268.6 billion provides more than a simple split-the-difference between Senate and House figures.

Reagan's defense-spending request for next fiscal year would be cut by roughly $12 billion, leaving an increase of $23 billion over anticipated defense spending for this year.

Speakes said the spending levels

See RESOLUTION
Back page, col. 1, this section

INSIDE

Staff Photo by Jim Gensheimer

Members of the Mod Quads of Monroeville, Pa., and of the Circle 8 of North Versailles, Pa., are in Louisville for a square dance convention this week. Yesterday they sat outside their trailers after lunch at the Kentucky Fair & Exposition Center.

Square dancers to give Louisville a whirl

30,000 do-si-do-ers will make convention Kentucky's largest

By LESLIE ELLIS
Courier-Journal Staff Writer

The square dance convention was three days away, but the Baileys and Fleshers and LaRoses, strangers until Sunday, had already set up camp at the fairgrounds. Yesterday, they were sharing drinks and becoming fast friends.

That's a square dancer for you. Outgoing, trusting.

"Instant camaraderie," said Michelle Bailey, her sunny, freckled face beaming at the group around her as the husbands pounded a picnic table together.

It's not long after the first "hello" that they'll invite you in for a soft drink or orange juice. (There's little liquor around. Did you ever try to "swing your partner" in a martini stupor?)

These folks are ready to dance at least eight hours a day this week, and the LaRoses, who describe themselves as young, crazy beginners, will probably be at it 12 hours a day.

Their swirls and high-stepping, with 60-year-olds moving as spritely as youngsters, will fill every corner of the Kentucky Fair & Exposition Center Thursday through Saturday. The anticipated attendance of 30,000 will make it the largest convention in Kentucky's history.

They're coming in cars, recreational vehicles and airplanes from all 50 states plus New Zealand, Japan, Germany, and even Saudi Arabia.

Some 600 callers, their voices a sing-song mixture of melody, agility and discipline, will lead the dancers through the intricate steps of square dancing, "contra" dances and clogging. From 9 a.m. to 1 a.m., there will be as many as 14 dances at one time.

For some, the 16 hours of organized dance at the convention isn't enough. Thirteen years ago, the

See SQUARE
Back page, col. 1, this section

Pope mentions Solidarity in speech to Polish miners

By MICHAEL DOBBS
© The Washington Post

KATOWICE, Poland — Pope John Paul II, speaking in Poland's industrial heartland, declared yesterday that God, not the state, has given workers the right to form free trade unions.

For the first time on his trip, the pope referred directly to the Solidarity trade federation that was outlawed by Poland's communist regime after the imposition of martial law in December, 1981.

Previously he had used "solidarity" only as a term for social unity.

The pope's words were greeted by cheering from an estimated crowd of 1.5 million people yesterday in Katowice, the capital of the coal-mining region of Silesia.

During a ceremony earlier yesterday in the western city of Poznan in Poland's agricultural belt, John Paul referred to Solidarity's companion organization, Rural Solidarity, which represented more than 1 million Polish farmers.

The pope's direct references to Solidarity, on the fifth day of his eight-day pilgrimage, emphasized his candor regarding his homeland's sensitive political issues.

In his speeches in Poland, he has called on the government to reopen a dialogue with society, and demanded respect for human rights and national sovereignty.

Government spokesman Jerzy Urban criticized the church on Sunday for failing to prevent "political manifestations" in connection with religious ceremonies attended by the pope.

John Paul tried to calm the crowds in Czestochowa Sunday evening by asking them to go home "in pious tranquillity" following Mass.

The pope's choice of Katowice to deliver his most detailed sermon yet on workers' rights was significant, because he wasn't allowed to visit the area during his first pilgrimage to Poland in June, 1979.

The Communist Party traditionally has tried to keep the miners, who are regarded as "the aristocrats of the working class," insulated from religious influence.

Nearly four decades of Marxist indoctrination, however, did not prevent miners and their families from gathering on a vast, abandoned air-

See POPE
Back page, col. 1, this section

Steam heat, summer treat

National Weather Service

LOUISVILLE area — Sunny, very warm and humid today and tomorrow. High today, upper 80s; tomorrow, near 90. Low tonight, mid-60s.

KENTUCKY — Mostly sunny, very warm and humid today, with a slight chance of thunderstorms east. Mostly sunny, very warm and humid tomorrow. Highs both days, mid- to upper 80s. Lows tonight, mid- to upper 60s.

INDIANA — Mostly sunny and hot today and tomorrow. Highs both days, 80s to 90. Lows tonight, 60s.

TENNESSEE — Partly cloudy west today, with widely scattered showers east. Partly cloudy tomorrow. Highs both days, 80s. Lows tonight, mid- to upper 60s.

High yesterday, 85; low, 64.
Year ago yesterday: High, 77; low, 52.
Sun: Rises, 6:20 EDT; sets, 9:09.
Moon: Rises, 5:49 p.m.; sets, 3:53 a.m.

Weather map and details, Page C 6.

Employers can't restrict workers' wives benefits, Supreme Court decides

From Los Angeles Times and AP Dispatches

WASHINGTON — It is illegal for employers to restrict the pregnancy or maternity benefits they pay to the wives of male workers, the Supreme Court ruled yesterday.

The court held, 7-2, that the federal Pregnancy Discrimination Act of 1978 provides protection not only to the women on a company's payroll but also to the wives of employees.

U.S. Chamber of Commerce officials complained that the decision will cost American businesses millions of dollars.

The ruling means that companies must pay for the costs of pregnancy and childbirth for the wives of working men, just as they pay other health expenses of their employees' spouses.

The justices struck down an insurance plan in which the Newport News Shipbuilding & Dry Dock Co. of Virginia paid all other hospital costs for employees' spouses, but paid no more than $500 toward the hospital expenses of pregnancy or childbirth.

"The 1978 act makes clear that it is discriminatory to treat pregnancy-related conditions less favorably than other conditions," Justice John Paul Stevens wrote for the court.

"Thus, (the shipping company's) plan unlawfully gives married male

See COURT
Back page, col. 4, this section

Residents, WKU fraternities are in tug of war over street

By CAROL MARIE CROPPER
Courier-Journal Staff Writer

BOWLING GREEN, Ky. — With the statue of Henry Hardin Cherry looking down from "The Hill," the battle over social acceptability being waged in the streets below seems almost ironic.

Cherry, himself, could not have predicted it.

During his tenure as the first president of what is now Western Kentucky University, he forbade fraternities and sororities because of their exclusive nature.

But fraternities and sororities arrived in the mid-1960s, almost three decades after his death in 1937.

But it's the fraternities and sororities that are now having problems being accepted.

The older people living in the two-story Victorian homes below the statue don't want the organizations in their neighborhood.

Homeowners complain about the noise and traffic that comes with fraternity parties. They complain about the empty beer kegs, the garbage and the damage they say is being done to the old homes.

"We call the police every 15 minutes some nights because it's so loud, and they urinate in our bushes," said Arthur "Corky" Gillis, who lives on College Street.

Bowling Green police say they get three or four complaints a night when the fraternity party season is at its peak — during fall rush, when new members are admitted.

Residents also complain about the fraternity parties on Thursday nights.

"By them being in a residential neighborhood, they're disturbing the neighbors," Maj. Elster Willoughby said.

Some older residents long for the days when the area had a different tone.

In "all these houses up and down here were proper people — people who were locally known," said Sam Rabold, a 74-year-old retired restaurant-owner.

"College Street was one of the best streets in Bowling Green."

The Greek houses changed that, he said.

Now "we are trying to do something to improve this neighborhood," said Suzanne Coombs, who lives in a turn-of-the century home — complete with Corinthian columns and leaded glass — with her dentist husband.

And improving the neighborhood, she said, hinges on keeping out additional fraternities.

The area being fought over — with the fraternities, sororities and university on one side, property owners on the other — is a cluster of tree-shaded streets on the northeastern edge of campus.

The neighborhood is studded with old two-story homes boasting such architectural confections as stained glass, carved pediments and fluted columns.

Sprinkled between — and in — such homes are apartment houses, fraternities and sororities. One former fraternity house stands vacant, boards nailed over the windows.

It is obviously a neighborhood in transition and has been so for years.

"If you go way back — back in the early '50s at least, that area went from large, general housing to taking in students," said John B. Matheney, planning director with the Bowling Green-Warren County Planning Commission.

"In the last few years, it's begun

See RESIDENTS
Back page, col. 1, this section

Photo by Kim Kolarik

Sam and Wilma Rabold of Bowling Green are upset that a fraternity might be moving in next door.

The Louisville Courier-Journal

Maintaining its tradition for being ranked among the nation's top newspapers was the *Courier-Journal,* which years ago earned the respect of eastern and midwestern editors who thought the South could not produce top-ranked publications. Since that time, of course, other papers have achieved national standing.

The *Courier-Journal* finished strongly enough in the "top 10" rankings and in the regional competition to be ranked high again. The paper finished ninth or tenth in five different regions in the "top 10" rankings and in a tie for sixth and seventh in the Mid-Atlantic states.

Henry Watterson ran the *Courier-Journal* from its beginning in 1868 until his retirement in 1919. A leading voice in the New South after the Civil War, Watterson was a prominent figure in American life who at times put his paper into the national spotlight. His retirement brought the Bingham family into the picture, first Judge Robert Worth Bingham, who bought the *Courier-Journal* and the *Times* in 1917, and later his son, Barry, who became directing owner of both papers.

It was Barry Bingham who brought Mark Ethridge to Louisville and later James S. Pope and Norman E. Isaacs. All four were vocal, intelligent leaders in journalism, managing the Louisville papers in various capacities and becoming known on a national scale. The *Courier-Journal* was Democratic in its political preferences, a progressive, fair-minded newspaper. Barry Bingham, Jr., became editor and publisher in 1971; Ethridge and Pope had retired, and Isaacs left to teach at Columbia University. Carol Sutton became managing editor in 1974, first woman to hold that post on a major daily. Two years later she was named assistant to young Bingham. The *Courier-Journal* won the 1967 Pulitzer Prize for public service, the judges citing a successful campaign to control the Kentucky strip mining industry and thus preserve the environment; the 1978 local reporting award; and the 1980 international award. Its daily circulation was approximately 180,000.

St. Petersburg Times

Florida's Best Newspaper

VOL. 99 — NO. 330   262 PAGES   ST. PETERSBURG, FLORIDA, SUNDAY, JUNE 19, 1983   50 CENTS A COPY

Feather Sound

7½ %

'Challenger' takes Ride into history

By ROBERT BARNES
St. Petersburg Times Staff Writer

CAPE CANAVERAL — Here are the historic words from America's first woman in space:

"Have you ever been to Disneyland?" she asked Mission Control in Houston. "That was definitely an E ticket."

Dr. Sally K. Ride, an astrophysicist from California, broke NASA's 22-year-old sex barrier when the gleaming white spaceship Challenger poked a hole in Earth's atmosphere Saturday and set out on a six-day mission. But Ride proved what she has said all along — that she is just an astronaut who happens to be a woman.

Forget the "one small step for woman" business. "See you Friday," she said instead.

Ride and the other four astronauts on the flight received their "E tickets" — that's what Walt Disney used to charge for his most extravagant amusements — at 7:33 Saturday morning. Challenger's rockets flared orange, the sun came from behind the clouds and shone brightly on the water, and the spaceship rolled into space, its vapor trail marking the sky like thick whipped cream.

THE LAUNCH was 59/1,000 of a second late. "We feel a little bad about that," joked Tom Hutsman, director of

Inside
■ Gasping in delight and snapping pictures like crazy, a half-million spectators watched as the shuttle Challenger blasted off, 6-A

■ In 1963 when the Soviets put the first woman in space, media sexism was a bit more unbridled, 6-A

■ Alan B. Shepard Jr., the first U.S. astronaut, now has a business career, 19-A

shuttle management and operations.

Challenger took off with the largest crew in NASA's history — a shuttle commander Robert L. Crippen, 45, pilot Frederick "Rick" Hauck, 42, and mission specialists Ride, 32, John M. Fabian, 44, and Dr. Norman Thagard, 39. All but Crippen are space rookies who joined the program in 1978, but Saturday's activities didn't give them much time to look out the windows.

The astronauts completed their first major task around 5 p.m. when they

launched a $40-million satellite for Telesat Canada, a private Canadian company. The communications satellite will increase telephone service in parts of that country and provide some viewers in the northern U.S. with pay-television channels.

The crew is scheduled to launch a similar satellite today for another paying customer, the Republic of Indonesia.

The 5-day, 23-hour, 30-minute mission, which is scheduled to end Friday morning

See SHUTTLE, 6-A

Sally Ride and fellow astronauts (left to right) Thagard, Fabian, Hauck and Crippen walk out early Saturday on their way to the shuttle ...

... and then blast off from Launch Pad 39-A in a flash of light and a cloud of smoke. Later, Ride asked ground controllers:

'Have you ever been to Disneyland? That was definitely an E ticket.'

St. Petersburg Times — TONY LOPEZ

---

inside

UPI reports that Billy Martin's job with the Yankees won't survive the weekend — 1-C

Trident submarine USS *Florida* is commissioned in Connecticut — 1-B

Guide to seeing Epcot, plus a review of Sea World's newest show — 1-E

McNulty Station is a fine example of rehabilitative architecture — 1-H

SECTION A	National, Foreign
SECTION B	Local, State
SECTION C	Sports
SECTION D	Perspective / Books
SECTION E	Arts / Travel
SECTION F	Family
SECTION G	Classified
SECTION H	Homes, Parts I and II
SECTION I	Business

Magazines: TV Dial, Parade

Antiques	9-H	Flea Market	8-H
Bridge	24-H	Health	2-F
Chess	25-H	Horoscope	6-F
Coins	23-H	Jumble	26-H
Computers	22-H	Landers	3-F
Condos	3-H	Sewing	4-F
Crossword	23-H	Stamps	23-H
Flarsheim	4-F	Wheels	20-H

Reagan reappoints Fed chief Volcker

By STEVEN R. WEISMAN
© New York Times

WASHINGTON — Ending months of speculation that has roiled the financial markets, President Reagan announced Saturday that he would reappoint Paul A. Volcker to another four-year term as chairman of the Federal Reserve Board.

Taking time from his regular Saturday radio address for what he said was "a news flash," Reagan told listeners that he telephoned Volcker Saturday morning and asked him to accept the reappointment.

"He's agreed to do so," the President said. "And I

couldn't be more pleased. He is as dedicated as I am to continuing the fight against inflation. And with him as chairman of the Fed, I know we'll win that fight."

Volcker's tight-money policies in 1981 and 1982 were credited by most economists with helping to bring down the nation's inflation rate and criticized by critics as causing the recession.

THE CHAIRMAN issued a statement saying he was "gratified and honored by the expression of confidence by the President."

Volcker was appointed chairman by President Jimmy Carter in 1979. His appointment to a new term beginning

Aug. 6 is subject to approval by the Senate, but he is not expected to have much difficulty winning confirmation.

In the regular Democratic response to Reagan's address, Sen. Thomas F. Eagleton of Missouri, said, "I vigorously support President Reagan's reappointment of Paul Volcker."

But another Democratic senator, Gary Hart of Colorado, who is seeking his party's presidential nomination, issued a statement saying that "to the degree this represents a continuation of the policies of the past two years," the selection "could be a disaster for our economy and for

See VOLCKER, 4-A

Cheers greet Pope as he uses word 'solidarity'

By KENNETH JAUTZ
Associated Press

CZESTOCHOWA, Poland — To the cheers of a million Poles, Pope John Paul II on Saturday hailed the workers' uprising that gave birth to the Solidarity labor movement, saying it touched the "hearts and consciences" of people around the world.

And for the first time since he began his Polish pilgrimage, the pontiff used the word "solidarity." The vast throng thundered back in joy.

Speaking to Polish youths at the medieval Jasna Gora monastery, the pontiff thanked his countrymen for their acts of "solidarity (with) those who were interned, imprisoned, dismissed from work, and also their families."

He used the word and as the trade union's name, but as a description of the spirit of resistance to martial law.

The Pope's remarks here were his strongest words of support for the banned Solidarity movement since returning to his native land Thursday.

John Paul, whose homecoming has touched off pro-Solidarity demonstrations wherever he has gone, was expected to meet in this southern town today with Lech Walesa, head of the outlawed union.

HIS FIRST ADDRESS here was made to members of the Baltic Diocese of Sarasota, his words booming out from a giant altar erected outside the monastery, whose

Pope meditates at monument to Warsaw Ghetto uprising.

See POPE, 4-A

Move to stop tax cut appears to be doomed

WASHINGTON — You may take this to the bank, Dear Reader: On July 1 — 12 days from today — your income taxes will go down.

ST. PETERSBURG TIMES
NATIONAL CORRESPONDENT

CHARLES STAFFORD

Sure, there has been talk of repealing or limiting the scheduled 10 percent cut in income tax rates, the third and last reduction in President Reagan's tax program approved by Congress in 1981. But it's not going to happen.

It is true that Thursday the House Ways and Means Committee approved Speaker Thomas P. "Tip" O'Neill's proposal to cap (limit) the tax cut for any tax return to no more than $720. But the vote was fragile, 18-15. Chairman Dan Rostenkowski, D-Ill., called the proposal a bad political maneuver.

Rep. Sam Gibbons of Tampa, the second-most-senior Democrat on the committee, called it "a symbolic gesture that is bound to fail." He was one of four Democrats who voted against it.

Two days before the committee approved the O'Neill bill, Gibbons was asked what Congress would do about the scheduled tax cut.

"NOTHING," HE SAID. "The committee will be forced to come out

with some kind of bill. The House will pass it. The Senate might pass it. But if it does, the President will veto it, and that will be that.

"You can spend yours. I've already spent mine."

But don't spend the whole thing. Remember this: While your personal income taxes are going down again, the federal tax you pay on a gallon of gasoline went up 5 cents last April, and the Social Security payroll tax is moving upward each year.

However, from the standpoint of federal taxes, you will be better off on Independence Day than you were five days earlier.

Talk of limiting the tax cut was a ploy of the Democratic leadership in Congress. The case for it was made in a recent special report by the Democratic

See TAXES, 11-A

The St. Petersburg Times

The second-ranked newspaper in the South, behind the *Miami Herald,* is the color-splashed *St. Petersburg* newspaper which first won attention under the direction of Nelson Poynter and later under Eugene C. Patterson. The survey results indicated the paper was far and away the favorite when it came to the "best designed" newspaper.

In the "top 5," the "St. Pete's" paper was seventh in the Deep South and eighth in the Mid-Atlantic states. It finished slightly ahead of the *Atlanta Constitution* to place second in the Deep South regional competition and ninth on region four's "top 10" list. The results showed that along with several other papers, there was enthusiasm for this newspaper.

Nelson Poynter was a fiercely independent newspaperman who in 1947 imposed upon himself "fifteen standards of ownership" which he published in his *St. Petersburg Times.* His dedication to high journalistic principles and basic liberalism helped him bring his paper into the top ranks of American dailies before his death in 1978.

The *Times* was founded in 1884 and came into Poynter family control in 1912. Nelson assumed direction in 1938. He and his wife, Henrietta, founded the objective research organization, *Congressional Quarterly,* in Washington, and bought control of their local competition in St. Petersburg, the *Evening Independent,* in 1962. Publishing an aggressive daily in a sleepy Florida city with 30 percent senior citizens was no mean feat, but the Poynters succeeded.

Poynter selected Eugene C. Patterson, who had left the *Atlanta Constitution* editorship in a 1968 dispute, to succeed him. Patterson came in 1972 and was in full control after 1978. The *Times* won the 1964 Pulitzer gold medal, a 1980 Pulitzer Prize for national reporting, and national acclaim for its graphics and spectacular color printing. Its stock was owned by the Modern Media Institute, a writing and coaching school which Poynter created to further journalistic standards, and under which Roy Peter Clark won a national reputation. Daily circulation was 235,000.

Newsday

THE LONG ISLAND NEWSPAPER ● TUESDAY, JUNE 28, 1983 ● 30 CENTS ● NASSAU

Accord Reached On Bond Issue

Assembly Passes Hiring Compromise;
Senate to Return to Albany for Vote

Page 5

TRAGIC RACE. U.S. balloonists Maxie Anderson, right, and Don Ida, shown at start of European race Sunday in Paris, were killed yesterday when their balloon crashed in West Germany. / **Page 4**

Connors during match with Kevin Curren

Connors Upset At Wimbledon

Sports Section

Newsday

Newsday, a Times Mirror holding, is one of the leading tabloids in the nation with a circulation of 525,000. Strong regional support—eighth in competitive region two—and sufficient national recognition pushed it into the top fifteen. Like some of the other papers mentioned in this grouping, *Newsday* is not mentioned as frequently as those papers in the top rankings. Yet it consistently produces solid coverage of its community and wins national prizes for its substantial national coverage.

Founded by Alicia Patterson in 1940 and controlled by her until her death in 1963, the paper won the Pulitzer Prize for public service in 1964 and 1970 for uncovering Long Island governmental scandals, and won another prize in 1974. Tom Darcy won the 1970 prize for cartooning.

Alicia Patterson and her husband, Harry F. Guggenheim, differed on politics, he being the more conservative. In presidential races the paper supported Democrats in 1956, 1960, and 1964 and Republicans in 1952 and 1968. The switch to Nixon in 1968 came after Guggenheim took control in 1963. His editors were Mark Ethridge, from Louisville, followed by Bill D. Moyers, President Johnson's press secretary, in 1966. Guggenheim apparently intended to put Moyers in control of *Newsday,* but became fearful of his policies and sold his 51 percent stock interest to Otis Chandler of the *Los Angeles Times* in 1970. Moyers resigned and William Attwood came from the Cowles magazines to head *Newsday* as publisher. David Laventhol was executive editor.

Under Otis Chandler's guidance, *Newsday,* by the early 1980s, was the second largest circulation evening daily. Donald Wright, chief operating officer after 1977, became the president and chief operating officer of the parent *Los Angeles Times* in 1982. Lou Schwartz succeeded Laventhol as executive editor in 1981.

SPECIAL TODAY

FOOD
Glorious grilling for summer

OPINION PAGE
The whys of insuring young drivers
Page 17

GREEN SHEET
How about checkout lane TV?

THE MILWAUKEE JOURNAL

Founded in 1882   Wednesday, June 15, 1983   Latest Edition I I

Abortion curbs rejected

Justices overturn 2nd-trimester restriction

AP and UPI

Washington, D.C. — The Supreme Court Wednesday struck down most state and local regulations making abortions more difficult to obtain, including a requirement that abortions for women more than three months pregnant be performed in licensed hospitals.

In three decisions resolving controversies over abortion regulation in Virginia, Missouri and Akron, Ohio, the court overturned as unconstitutional infringements of women's rights to privacy any regulations requiring:

Women to receive abortions in full-service hospitals after pregnancy has reached the second trimester, or second three months.

Doctors to tell women seeking abortions about possible birth-giving alternatives and also to tell them a fetus is "a human life."

Doctors to wait at least 24 hours after a woman signs an abortion consent form before performing the procedure.

The justices said, however, that states and communities may require that second-trimester abortions be performed in licensed abortion clinics or so-called outpatient hospitals.

At least 21 states require that such abortions be performed in full-service hospitals.

[In Wisconsin, the State Medical Examining Board has ruled that second-trimester abortions must be done in licensed hospitals. However, Federal Judge Barbara C. Crabb postponed enactment of the rule pending the Supreme Court's judgment in the three cases decided Wednesday.]

In the Missouri case, the court upheld portions of a state law requiring the presence of a second physician during abortions for women in their last three months of pregnancy; requiring minors to get the consent of a parent or a judge before obtaining an abortion, and requiring a pathology report for every abortion performed.

The court's rulings on each regulation at issue were reached by various coalitions of justices, most of them led by Justice Lewis F. Powell.

The decisions marked the first
Turn to **Court, Page 13**

Sex film shown to wrong class

By David I. Bednarek
Journal Education Reporter

A film about conception and birth, intended for sixth, seventh and eighth graders, caused a stir at Milwaukee's 78th Street School last week when it was accidentally shown to a second grade class.

The mother of a boy in the class complained about the film, saying it forced her to talk to her son about conception and birth years before she intended to do so.

The mother, who is a nurse, asked that her name not be used in the story. She said her son, after seeing the film, asked her several questions about the vagina, sperm and penis.

"I had to explain the whole facts of life to him," she said. "I had to tell him everything, physical coupling and all. And his kindergarten sister knows, too, which is sad."
Turn to **Film, Page 14**

Police union, city close to agreement

By Paul Bargren
of The Journal Staff

The City of Milwaukee and its police union are close to agreement on a new contract, representatives of both sides say.

A settlement may be reached at a negotiating session set for 9 a.m. next Tuesday at the Park East Hotel, said James Geissner, city labor negotiator.

In an interview Wednesday, Bill Krueger, head of the Milwaukee Police Association, said:

"We're close. It doesn't look like arbitration will be needed."

Krueger said the last time the police union and the city agreed on a contract without arbitration or a strike was the 1975-'76 contract.

Krueger said the main issues in the new contract were overtime, health insurance payments for retirees and uninsured motorist insurance for officers on duty.

While parity between firefighters and police officers has been a hot issue in the past, it is not a top priority in this round of talks, Krueger said.

He said officers would like more paid overtime and less compensatory
Turn to **Police, Page 13**

Rainstorms clear air of unhealthy ozone

The rain that fell Tuesday afternoon reduced ozone levels in the air to acceptable levels as it poured on rush-hour traffic, dropping as much as an inch in Bayside.

Long-range prospects indicate that the Milwaukee area may be high and dry from Thursday through Saturday, the National Weather Service says.

The ozone alert, which indicated unhealthful conditions, was called for five southeastern Wisconsin counties Monday afternoon but was lifted 24 hours later when the downpour arrived, according to the State Department of Natural Resources.

Mild weather is expected Friday through Sunday, with daytime highs in the upper 70s and nighttime lows in the upper 50s. There will be a chance of showers and thunderstorms "about Sunday," the weather service says.

The rain Tuesday measured about a third of an inch at Mitchell Field but was much heavier in the northern suburbs. The high temperature Tuesday was 83.

PARK PLANNED — The vacant land in the center of this picture, at Water St. and Wisconsin Ave., will become a park — at least for a few years. The picture was taken Wednesday from the Marine Bank building.
—Journal Photo by John E. Biever

On, Wisconsin

An Editorial

Curtailing disparity in sentences

The Wisconsin Supreme Court should order statewide use of sentencing guidelines, as recommended by a committee headed by Milwaukee Chief Judge Victor Manian. As Manian said, a statewide test could help allay citizens' concerns about seeming variations in sentencing.

Manian told the high court that, in an 18-month test, 55% of judges in eight counties voluntarily applied the guidelines in sentencing for specified offenses. He said the test did not disclose wide variations in sentences.

It's important to have some predictability about sentencing. It's also important to maintain judicial discretion. The guidelines, which help preserve discretion and provide some predictability, weigh such considerations as the severity of the offense, a defendant's prior criminal record and mitigating and aggravating factors in the case. Under the new statewide 18-month test sought by Manian's committee, judges who did not use the guidelines would have to explain their refusal to do so.

Guidelines represent an alternative to the rigid mandatory or determinate sentences that some people would like to see the Legislature impose. Lawmakers should consider the high cost of required, fixed sentences. In several states, mandatory and determinate sentences have caused chaos in the prison systems.

Sentencing guidelines might not eliminate disparities in the treatment of similarly situated defendants, but it would minimize them — while preserving judicial discretion to consider individual factors. The Supreme Court should permit use of the guidelines throughout the state.

Firsts in space

1961	First man orbits Earth — Yuri Gagarin, USSR
	First woman in space — Valentina Tereshkova, USSR
'65	First spacewalk — Alexey Leonov, USSR
'68	First manned flight to moon orbit — Apollo 8, USA
'69	Man's first walk on moon — Neil Armstrong, USA
'73	Skylab 4 crew sets US endurance record of 84 days
'75	First US-Soviet link in space
'80	Endurance record of 185 days set by Soyuz 35 crew, USSR
'81	First reusable spacecraft tested — Columbia, USA
1983	First American woman in space — Sally Ride

Source: The Associated Press

ANOTHER MILESTONE — When Sally Ride goes into space aboard the US shuttle Challenger Saturday, she will become the first American woman in space. Ride and her four crewmates were flying from Houston to Cape Canaveral, Fla., Wednesday to prepare for the six-day mission. Launch time is 6:33 a.m. CDT Saturday.

Carleys delay project; park planned instead

By Fran Bauer
of The Journal Staff

The hole in the ground at the northwest corner of Water St. and Wisconsin Ave., once planned as the site of a 29-story office building, will be landscaped and turned into a park for two or three years, it was announced Wednesday.

A lack of sufficient demand for commercial space makes it necessary to delay the office project, said George Mitchell, president of the Carley Management Co. of Madison, in a brief press release, Mitchell described the landscaping as an interim measure to last until market conditions improve.

In mid-1980, developers David and James Carley unveiled a plan to build an office building called River Place on the site, where Solomon Juneau, a founder of Milwaukee, built his first log cabin in 1818. The cabin was Milwaukee's first building. The 14-story Pabst building was razed by the Carleys to make way for the project.

After the Carleys announced their plan for River Place, however, their firm was selected by the federal government to build the new Reuss Federal Plaza, now nearing completion at 310 W. Wisconsin Ave. Rising interest rates increased the cost of constructing the Federal Plaza 75%, Mitchell said.

In addition, high interest rates and the weak economy have lessened demand for new office space in Milwaukee, he said.

River Place also was facing competition in the Downtown office market.

The Wausau Co., a real estate and development subsidiary of the Seattle-based SAFECO Insurance Co., is building a 30-story office building at 411 E. Wisconsin Ave. IBM has signed a long-
Turn to **Park, Page 14**

The Weather

National Weather Service

Milwaukee — Partly cloudy tonight, 30% chance of showers early; low mid-50s. Partly sunny Thursday; high low to mid-70s.

Hour	3	4	5	6	7	8	9	10	11	12
Temp.	64	63	59	58	59	65	69	72	74	76

Wisconsin — Partly cloudy tonight, chance of showers or thunderstorms early; lows mid-40s to low 50s. Partly sunny Thursday; highs upper 60s to mid-70s. Weather map, Page 12.

The Milwaukee Journal

Survey respondents apparently knew of the *Journal's* tradition as a conscientiously edited, community-conscious paper. The paper garnered enough support, particularly from its section of the nation where it was eleventh on the "top 10" list, to be included in the top fifteen newspapers. The *Journal* has long been a favorite of professional journalists, enjoying a solid reputation. Its editorial page often was ranked along with those of the *Washington Post, St. Louis Post-Dispatch,* and comparable newspapers.

The *Journal,* which dates to 1882, was led by Lucius W. Nieman, who as publisher set high standards for community coverage. Under his guidance the paper developed an international stance, supporting the League of Nations and later the United Nations. There were serious clashes with fellow Wisconsinites, including the LaFollettes who favored isolationism and Milwaukee's Socialist leader, Victor Berger. Normally Democratic, the *Journal* switched to Willkie in 1940 and Dewey in 1948. Its battle with Senator Joseph R. McCarthy helped cause McCarthy to lose the city of Milwaukee while he was winning reelection in 1952, during the height of the Korean War. That fierce fight brought the paper more nationwide attention as a defender of liberties.

Another prominent name in *Journal* history is that of Harry J. Grant, who acquired the title of publisher in 1919. It was Grant who brought Marvin H. Creager from the *Kansas City Star,* and Creager, as managing editor and later as editor and company president, reinforced the *Journal's* local coverage and writing qualities with an insistence born of his *Star* experience.

Nieman died in 1935 and his wife in 1936. Part of the Nieman fortune was left to Harvard University, which used it to establish the Nieman Fellowships for newspapermen. The Nieman stock holdings in the paper were up for sale, but Grant saved the situation by organizing an employee-ownership plan similar to that of the *Star* in Kansas City. Grant, as board chairman and a substantial stockholder, remained in firm control. J. Donald Ferguson succeeded Creager as editor in 1943, giving way to Lindsay Hoben in 1961.

Richard H. Leonard became managing editor in 1962 and moved up to the editorship in 1967 on the death of Hoben. John Reddin and Sig Gis-

On Today's Editorial Page
Who Decides At City Hospital? *Editorial*
The Challenger Returns *Editorial*

ST. LOUIS POST-DISPATCH

FINAL ★ ★
Latest Stock Prices Pages 4B and 5B

Vol. 105, No. 176 — MONDAY, JUNE 27, 1983 — Copyright 1983 25'

States' Tax On Corporations Upheld

Compiled From News Services

WASHINGTON — The Supreme Court handed states a dollars-and-cents victory today, ruling that they may tax part of the total worldwide income of multinational corporations that do business within the state.

The justices also agreed today to consider modifying the court's 69-year-old "exclusionary rule" that bars illegally obtained evidence from being used in criminal trials.

In another action, the court let stand a decision that the use of trained dogs to sniff out drugs on students is unconstitutional.

In the ruling on multinational corporations, the justices voted 5-3 to uphold a California law that levies taxes on that part of the overall income of a corporation and its foreign subsidiaries that is attributable to the parent company's operations within state boundaries. The law is similar to those in 22 other states, including Illinois but not Missouri.

Writing for the court, Justice William J. Brennan Jr. rejected assertions that the practice, termed double taxation by the corporations, invites retaliation by foreign nations against U.S. companies abroad.

FOUR JUSTICES favor relaxing rules on evidence. Page 11A

Corporations had argued such taxation is unfair because they should have to pay no state taxes on income earned abroad by foreign subsidiaries. But the states maintain that it prevents giant corporations from avoiding taxes by shuffling profits among subsidiaries.

Hopes among Justice Department officials and law enforcement officers that the justices would relax the "exclusionary rule" of criminal evidence were revived when the justices agreed to consider a "good faith" exception to it.

The exclusionary rule, which bars illegally seized evidence from being used in criminal trials, is often blamed for allowing guilty persons to go free on legal technicalities.

The justices agreed today to hear arguments next term in cases from Massachusetts, California and Colorado that each ask the justices to forgive honest mistakes that technically make a search illegal.

The Massachusetts case is an appeal of a ruling that blood-stained evidence found in a murder suspect's home should not have been admitted in his trial.

The California case is an appeal of federal court rulings that bar evidence of cocaine and other narcotics from being used as evidence against four accused drug traffickers.

The lower courts said the evidence could not be used at trial because Burbank, Calif., police illegally searched two houses and several cars to uncover the drugs. The courts declared the searches illegal even though police had a warrant.

According to the lower courts, the problem was that police had no solid reasons to suspect a crime and should have been denied a warrant. Police sought the warrant after getting a tip from an informant and after watching the suspects' activities for one month.

In the Colorado case, the state court found that police had arrested Fidel Quintero illegally without strong enough reasons to suspect him of a crime. Applying the exclusionary rule, it said none of the stolen goods Quintero had been carrying could be used against him at a new trial.

In the case involving sniff-searches, the justices refused to hear arguments

See COURT, Page 5

Gary Bohn/Post-Dispatch

Japanese Kites

Visitors to the Japanese Festival at Shaw's Garden Sunday saw this display of Oriental kites. The festival, which ended Sunday, featured samples of Japanese art and culture.

Waste 'Superfund' Becomes State Law

By Marjorie Mandel
Of the Post-Dispatch Staff

Missouri will have its own "Superfund" to deal with hazardous waste as a result of a bill signed today by Gov. Christopher S. Bond.

The fund is expected to raise from $3.1 million to $4 million a year from additional fees on generators of hazardous waste.

Its approval in the last session of the Legislature had been spurred by the discovery of 31 sites in the state contaminated by the toxic chemical dioxin.

"This is an important day for Missouri," Bond said at a signing ceremony at the Wainwright State Office Building, 111 North Seventh Street.

"With enactment of the state Superfund law, we have now provided a crucial means for dealing with the dangers of hazardous waste, which we live with now and which threaten our future."

Bond noted that Missouri was one of the first states to have created such a fund.

"The national attention focused on Missouri's dioxin crisis has not always been pleasant but I think Missourians can be proud of the fact that we are emerging as a national leader in the management of hazardous waste problems," he said.

The Superfund's sponsor, state Rep. Bob Feigenbaum, D-Ferguson, said the law showed that "we could take a very negative situation and turn it around to a very positive situation."

Also joining Bond at the signing were Fred A. Lafser, director of the state Department of Natural Resources; Marilyn L. Leistner, mayor of dioxin-contaminated Times Beach; residents of the so-called Minker and Stout dioxin sites in northern Jefferson County.

Also present were representatives of the Associated Industries of Missouri, the Monsanto Co., the Missouri Bus and Truck Association, the Coalition for the Environment and the Missouri Public Interest Research Group.

The Superfund is designed to finance the cleanup of about 60 hazardous waste sites, including the dioxin sites, across the state.

The new law also:

— Increases liability of those

See SUPERFUND, Page 5

Dumping Of Dioxin Into River Studied

By Laszlo K. Domjan
Of the Post-Dispatch Staff
Copyright, 1983, St. Louis Post-Dispatch

Environmental officials are taking a closer look at a now-defunct chemical company that they believe dumped dioxin into the Mississippi River at St. Louis in the 1960s.

They want to know whether the plant site formerly occupied by Thompson Chemicals Corp. at the foot of Chouteau Avenue may be contaminated by the chemical. They also are considering testing fish in the Mississippi to see if any dioxin remains in the river.

Dr. Coleman Carter, a former medical investigator for the federal Centers for Disease Control in Atlanta, learned about Thompson's dumping in 1974.

Dr. Carter at the time was trying to trace the source of dioxin that poisoned three horse arenas in Missouri in 1971. He wanted to know which dioxin producer had hired Russell M. Bliss, the waste oil dealer from west St. Louis County who had spread dioxin-tainted oil on the arena floors.

Officials suspect the Thompson plant produced dioxin as a byproduct. Former employees assured Dr. Carter that the company would have had no reason to hire Bliss to dispose of it. Dr. Carter was told that Thompson had a cost-free method of waste disposal outside its gates — the Mississippi River.

"I was told that they had been dumping their wastes directly into the river," Dr. Carter said. Such dumping at that time would not have been illegal.

Dr. Carter eventually identified the maker of the dioxin sprayed in the arenas as a defunct chemical producer in southwestern Missouri.

The Thompson Chemical company went out of business in 1970 and the

See THOMPSON, Page 12

Post-Dispatch graphic by Tony Lazorko

EPA Keeps On Payroll 7 Who Quit

WASHINGTON (UPI) — Because of the controversy surrounding the Environmental Protection Agency, seven of 21 political appointees left their jobs. But they didn't really leave the agency.

Most of the officials were asked to resign policy-making jobs. They now are serving as temporary government consultants. They earn more than $240 a day, a cost of about $100,000 to taxpayers.

In one case, White House officials are alleged to have pressed new EPA Director William D. Ruckelshaus to keep on board the former administrator of the agency's regional office in San Francisco because of her loyal campaign support for President Ronald Reagan, EPA sources said. The administrator, Sonia Crow, now is earning $245 a day as a consultant. She will draw about $14,500 over a 60-day period.

In finding positions for the officials

See EPA, Page 12

Pentecostal Family Leaves Russia After 23-Year Fight

Compiled From News Services

MOSCOW — A Siberian Pentecostal family left the Soviet Union today, ending a 23-year struggle to emigrate that took family members through prison, labor camps and nearly five years in the basement of the U.S. Embassy in Moscow.

Pyotr and Augustina Vashchenko, their 12 children and their daughter-in-law boarded a Pan Austrian Airlines for Vienna, Austria, this morning — five years to the day after members of the family burst into the U.S. Embassy seeking refuge.

"We want to thank everybody who helped us. We want to thank the Soviet, the American and the Israeli governments," Pyotr Vashchenko said at Sheremetyevo-2 Airport in Moscow.

"We hope the Americans will make some kind of gesture," he said. He did not elaborate, but the Soviets apparently will expect reciprocal action of some kind in exchange for allowing the Vashchenkos to leave the country.

American diplomats have refused to confirm or deny that a deal had been negotiated with Soviet authorities to allow the Vashchenkos to leave the country.

For the Vashchenkos, it was the end of a 23-year battle to emigrate.

"We feel great," Pyotr's daughter Lyuba said.

She said the family had been granted exit visas last Thursday in the Siberian town of Chernogorsk. Family members traveled by train for four days before reaching Moscow Sunday night.

The Vashchenkos sold a family cow and their house to raise the fees for their visas, which cost $1,000 each for the adults and about $360 for the two

See PENTECOSTAL, Page 8

7 Months Of Planning Readies VP Fair To Meet Emergencies

By Robert L. Koenig
Of the Post-Dispatch Staff

Danny Rideout had a heart attack in the midst of a million people.

As he was walking down the steps below the Gateway Arch on July 5, 1982, the final day of the VP Fair, he felt sharp pains in his chest. All the streets in the riverfront area were closed. The area around Rideout was jammed with fair-goers.

But emergency volunteers at the fair began treating Rideout within minutes at a first-aid station. He was evacuated from the crowded Arch grounds, taken to a nearby hospital and was back at work in six weeks.

"I guess I was going to have a heart attack no matter where I was," Rideout said. "And, looking back, I'd say it couldn't have happened in a better place — a few steps from the first-aid trailer. It may have saved my life."

Rideout's case was unusual — most of the medical problems at last year's fair involved heat

See VP FAIR, Page 4

Pro-American Party Keeps Control In Japanese Election

Compiled From News Services

TOKYO — Prime Minister Yasuhiro Nakasone's Liberal-Democratic Party on Sunday swept parliamentary elections, assuring his administration a strong hand in its efforts to strengthen Japan's defense and forge closer ties with Washington.

Official returns showed that the pro-American, pro-business party won 68 out of the 126 seats contested in the House of Councillors — a gain of three seats in the upper house of the Diet, or parliament.

The conservative Liberal-Democratic Party already held 69 seats that will not be up for election until 1986. Altogether, the party has 137 of 252 seats in the house, giving it complete control of the upper chamber.

The Socialist Party, its primary challenger, trailed with 22 seats, a loss of four. The rest of the seats up for election were shared by a number of smaller parties.

The Liberal-Democrats enjoyed a majority of 134 before Sunday's voting. The Socialists held 48 seats, Komeito — the "Clean Government Party" — held 27, the Japan Communist Party 12 and the Democratic Socialists 12. The remaining posts were shared by smaller political groups.

The outcome of the election, held every three years, did not directly affect the incumbent administration, which has advocated strengthened ties with Washington, but represented the first test of the 65-year-old Nakasone's popularity and policies since he took office last November.

"From now on, my aim (is) to pursue cautious politics with greater modesty and with an open mind, by

See JAPAN, Page 8

MONDAY

Weather

Rain

Official forecast for St. Louis and vicinity: Fifty percent chance of thunderstorms tonight and tomorrow. Low tonight near 70, high tomorrow in the low to mid 80s. Chance for showers Wednesday. Highs Wednesday through Friday in the mid 80s to low 90s and lows, in the mid to upper 60s.

Other Weather on Page 3A

Inside

42 Pages

Features

WAR GAMES: The Air Force stages a flying rodeo to see whether its troops (right) are on target. Page 1D of Everyday

Business

STORE WARS: Some groceries that followed Kroger into "double couponing" two months ago are showing signs of tiring. Page 1B of Business Today

Nation

RECORD CREST: The Colorado River, already 2½ feet above its 11-foot flood stage in Grand Junction, Colo., may rise another foot or more today. Page 6A

Local

COCKTAIL DRESS TO KHAKI: Miss Israel, here for the Miss Universe pageant, will be drafted into the military in February. Page 3A

sler edited the editorial pages and Joseph W. Shoquist became managing editor. The *Journal* won the 1967 Pulitzer Prize for public service, repeating its 1918 award, and also the 1977 local reporting prize. Its employees owned 80 percent of the stock in the Journal Company, which also owned the *Milwaukee Sentinel* and the city's major television station. Daily circulation was 308,000.

The St. Louis Post-Dispatch

The St. Louis paper, although slipping in circulation along with a number of other evening newspapers, also was an appropriate choice. One of those old favorites of an older generation of newspaper buffs, the *Post-Dispatch* is a regional favorite with enough national appeal to keep a position in the top fifteen, precarious as it might be.

Founded in 1878 by Joseph Pulitzer and edited from 1911 to 1955 by the second Joseph Pulitzer—and since then by the third in that line, Joseph Pulitzer III—the paper has that romantic tie to journalism history. Continuity, both of Pulitzer family ownership and of the *Post-Dispatch* editorial policies, proved to be the key to greatness.

O. K. Bovard, one of America's great newsmen, provided the necessary complement of leadership during his thirty years as *Post-Dispatch* managing editor, from 1908 to 1938. Under his tutelage, such brilliant reporters as Paul Y. Anderson, Charles G. Ross, Marquis Childs, and Raymond P. Brandt advanced from St. Louis to the Washington scene to help win a national reputation for the paper. Anderson proved to be the mainspring of Bovard's effort after World War I to expand *Post-Dispatch* coverage of the national scene. Anderson and his paper were the first to realize the significance of the Teapot Dome scandal.

What the *Post-Dispatch* called the "dignity page"—the opening page of the traditionally liberal editorial section—was developed by Bovard to carry special articles on political, economic, scientific, and cultural subjects. When Bovard resigned in 1938 after differences with his publisher, Benjamin H. Reese became managing editor. Raymond L. Crowley succeeded Reese in 1951.

The *Post-Dispatch* won five Pulitzer Prize gold medals for meritorious public service during the fifteen years beginning in 1937. Politically, *Post-Dispatch* support had usually been given to Democratic presidential candidates, although it deserted Roosevelt once, in 1936, and supported Dewey in 1948. It opposed Richard Nixon in his three presidential races, giving George McGovern positive support in 1972.

Crowley's retirement in 1962 brought Arthur R. Bertelson to the managing editorship; when he advanced to executive editor, Evarts A

Seventh shuttle flight has share of firsts

By Charles Seabrook
Staff Writer

The seventh space shuttle launch, now set for 7:33 a.m. Saturday, should be old hat to Americans by now.

But the National Aeronautics and Space Administration has again managed to pique the public's interest sky high, the same way NASA has on all other shuttle flights since the first voyage in April 1980.

NASA keeps the nation's attention by emphasizing "firsts" on each trip, such as the first launching of a satellite, on the fifth flight, and the first spacewalk from a shuttle, on the sixth flight.

Saturday's shuttle launch will have

■ Challenger is being groomed for launch and "all activities is the countdown were either on or ahead of schedule," NASA says. Page 3-A

its fair share of original events. The chief attraction is Sally Ride, who will be the first American woman to travel into space. Newspapers and television broadcasts across the nation have focused on the 31-year-old physicist.

She will be one of five crew members on the shuttle, marking another first — the first time the space vehicle has carried five persons.

Perhaps more significant to NASA officials is another sew event on

flight No. 7 — the landing of the shuttle on the 3-mile-long runway at Kennedy Space Center. The landing, set for 6:53 a.m. June 24, has had to take a back seat to the media hoopla about Ms. Ride.

"None of these 'firsts' has been planned as publicity stunts," said Mark Hess, NASA spokesman at Kennedy Space Center. "For one thing, Bob Crippen commander of the seventh shuttle voyage) asked for Sally Ride to be on this trip. NASA regards her as just another one of the troops that will be on board Saturday."

NASA is quick to point out, however, that Crippen is the first astronaut

See SHUTTLE, Page 8-A

'Firsts' on the shuttle

The space shuttle Challenger   The Associated Press

■ First U.S. woman in space.

■ Largest shuttle crew — five.

■ First landing on East Coast.

■ Second flight for commander.

---

a.m. NEWSBANK
VOL. 115, NO. 337 ☐ 108 PAGES-8 SECTIONS

THE ATLANTA CONSTITUTION

SPORTS FINAL   FRIDAY, JUNE 17, 1983   25 CENTS

★★★ Copyright © 1983 The Atlanta Constitution

Klansmen charged in death
Two Ku Klux Klansmen were charged Thursday in Mobile, Ala., in the 1981 beating death of a black teenager whose body was left hanging from a tree on a city street. One quickly pleaded guilty. 6-A.

Blackout hits airport

Car hits pole; thousands left without power

By Dick Parker
Staff Writer

A motorist who hit a utility pole in East Point late Thursday knocked out power to much of the southern metropolitan area, including Hartsfield International Airport.

Georgia Power spokesman Dave Altman said 4,000 to 6,000 Georgia Power customers lost electricity immediately after the accident. About half of East Point, whose residents got power indirectly from Georgia Power, were also left in the dark, East Point police said.

The car struck a power pole at 11 p.m. near Baird Street and Willingham Drive in East Point, knocking out power to Hapeville and Fort McPherson as well as Hartsfield and major portions of East Point.

Altman said a vehicle struck a guy wire and severed it. "The wire flipped up into the transmission wire, and that shorted out the whole thing," he said.

The transmission line, which was near a large Georgia Power substation, carried 115,000 volts to serve the East Point and south Atlanta areas, Altman said.

By 1:30 a.m. power had been restored to most of the affected areas. Georgia Power crews were still working to restore power to other affected areas.

Power lost at Hartsfield left the airport in darkness for seconds before emergency power was started, according to Delta Air Lines Operations Coordinator Ralph Bailey.

"The lights flashed, then flashed again, then went totally off," Bailey said. He said an emergency power source took over immediately.

"All air traffic controllers had full auxiliary power, Bailey said, and no contact was lost with any airplanes. "The controllers are not in the dark," he said. "And the runways are totally lit. We're in good shape. We never lost power to the runway."

See BLACKOUT, Page 8-A

Andropov consolidates his power
Tightening his grip on power in the Kremlin, Communist Party chief Yuri Andropov became president of the Soviet Union Thursday, completing his acquisition of the late Leonid Brezhnev's posts. 10-A.

Plane crash kills 14
All 14 men aboard a U.S. Navy patrol plane were killed when the aircraft plowed into a ridge on the rugged northern coast of the island of Kauai, Hawii, while on a routine training mission. Officials said the P-3 Orion plane was from the 'Screaming Eagles' Patrol Squadron One. 2-A.

A bird . . . a plane . . . a joke
"Superman III" is an out-and-out comic book. The director has given us a big-screen "Batman" episode, says film critic Eleanor Ringel. Christopher Reeve is still marvelous in his dual role as classic under-and-over achiever rolled into one. He has a wonderful time playing Superman as a Creep of Steel. 1-B.

CALVIN CRUCE/Staff

Safe from fire
Ansley Pascoli hugs her great-aunt Mary Winn, a resident of the Buckhead high-rise for the elderly, where a fire was sparked by a cigarette lighter. Ms. Pascoli came to check on her great-aunt after the fire that killed one and injured 16. Page 25-A.

Aid for Israel cost U.S. $24 billion

By James McCartney
Knight-Ridder Newspapers

WASHINGTON — Official American aid to Israel through 1982 has totaled more than $24 billion, a figure substantially larger than previous public estimates by the government, according to the secret draft report of a study by the General Accounting Office.

The GAO report also describes a number of previously undisclosed special favors by American administrations to Israel that go far beyond those extended by the United States to any other country.

According to the study, these favors

have ranged from exempting the Israelis from normal requirements to report how U.S. money has been spent to outright gifts of millions of dollars worth of American equipment — in one instance valued at $172 million.

The report also discloses that the United States has granted far more favorable terms for repaying loans than other countries enjoy, a persistent winking at enforcement of U.S. laws where Israel is involved, and a pattern of allowing Israel freedom of action, even when Israeli actions have contradicted stated U.S. policies.

The $24 billion in military and economic aid from the time of Israel's birth in 1948 through 1982, if added to sums approved by Congress through fiscal 1984, brings the total thus far committed to Israel to about $29 billion — a little more than $7,000 for every living Israeli.

Previously, the highest estimates of combined economic and military aid by members of Congress familiar with the program have been in the $20 billion range.

The GAO, a congressional watchdog

See ISRAEL, Page 11-A

Inside
■ Sirhan Sirhan, the assassin of Sen. Robert F. Kennedy, is denied parole. 20-A.
■ The Senate rejects a pay raise to $100,000, then OKs a hike to $69,800 immediately. 7-A.
■ ABC's lineup this fall will be as trashy as ever, says television columnist John Carman. 1-C.

Still hot
It will be sunny in Atlanta Friday with a 30 percent chance of thundershowers. High in the upper 80s. Details, 14-C.

AFGHANISTAN:
THE TWO FACES OF WAR

Kabul life appears normal, but fight is never far away

■ Our Washington bureau chief Andrew Glass journeyed from Moscow to Kabul for a rare look by an American reporter at the war as it is being fought from the communist side. Here, in the sixth of a series of articles on Afghanistan, is our reporter on the scene in the Afghan capital.

By Andrew J. Glass
Cox News Service

KABUL, Afghanistan

This ancient crossroads of civilization is now a garrison city. Soviet-built olive-drab jeeps and army trucks roll by squat armored personnel carriers from which Russian troops guard the major thoroughfares.

On Kabul's streets, already scorching hot by mid-May, traffic moves at a frantic pace. A blue-and-white Hungarian-made bus blows diesel fumes onto turbaned Kabulis as they hang on from every open window. A battered yellow-and-white taxi boldly passes a gleaming black Mercedes with government plates.

Poorer Afghans get around on bicycles or on donkeys. The poorest walk — the women among them covered head-to-toe in olive-dyed chuddars, slit only by a dense

JOSEPH ALBRIGHT/Special

Kabul streets: Animals, machines vie for space

fishnet at eye-level.

Jeeps and tanks, cars and trucks, bicycles and carts, wheelbarrows and donkeys, all vie with flocks of sheep for space on Kabul's dusty streets — creating a cacophony of machines, men and animals.

In many ways, life in Kabul appears normal. What is not normal is the drone of military helicopters, the boom

See KABUL, Page 12-A

50,000 march to greet pope, criticize regime

By Andrew J. Glass
Cox News Service

WARSAW — As church bells rang out through the country, Pope John Paul II returned Thursday to his native Poland, offering his troubled flock "a kiss of peace." The emotional pilgrimage prompted more than 50,000 to march on Communist Party headquarters.

In kneeling to kiss "my native soil" at Okecie airport and in riding through crowded Warsaw streets in his

■ So far, 1,373 Solidarity activists and their families have chosen one-way tickets out of Poland and uncertain lives in the United States. Page 8-A.

raised, bulletproof "popemobile," John Paul sought to heal the wounds caused by civil strife and hardship in this profoundly Catholic country.

The tense, emotional visit caused a spontaneous demonstration in support of the outlawed Solidarity labor movement, which the pontiff has backed.

In defiance of government warnings, the mass march began outside St. John's Cathedral following the pope's homily at a memorial ceremony for the late Polish primate Cardinal Stefan Wyszynski.

As the huge crowd — the biggest unofficial gathering here since martial law was declared 1½ years ago — marched past Communist Party headquarters on Jerozolimskie Avenue, they taunted the Polish ZOMO riot police with yells of "ZOMO go to work!"

See POPE, Page 8-A

Graham, Jr., succeeded him. Raymond P. Brandt retired in 1967 after forty-four years in the Washington bureau; Marquis Childs, his successor as bureau chief, won the 1970 Pulitzer Prize for commentary before retirement. Richard Dudman replaced him to become another outstanding Washington bureau chief for the *Post-Dispatch*. William F. Woo was editorial page chief and Thomas Englehardt, cartoonist. Circulation had declined sharply by the early 1980s, like that of other afternoon dailies, but the *Post-Dispatch* still won the plaudits of a *Wall Street Journal* reporter for having the spirit "to say what it thinks" in traditional liberal stance. The circulation was 237,000.

The Atlanta Constitution

Another long-time voice in the South, the *Constitution* kept pace with competitors in the survey. In past surveys the paper was included in the list of the nation's top publications and the tradition has been maintained. It is appropriate that Atlanta is represented, because the city gave the South two strong newspapers, the *Constitution* and the *Journal.* In the "top 10" rankings the paper was seventh in the Southwest, eighth in New England, and tenth in the Deep South.

Clark Howell, Sr., who succeeded Henry Grady at the *Constitution* in 1889, became the paper's owner and served as editor until 1936. His son, Clark Howell, Jr., named Ralph McGill as editor in 1938. McGill opposed the Ku Klux Klan and the Talmadge political machine in Georgia and won a Pulitzer Prize for editorial writing in 1959. James M. Cox, owner of the *Journal,* obtained control of the *Constitution* in 1950, but the papers continued to have separate editorial policies. When McGill became a syndicated columnist and publisher of the *Constitution* in 1960, Eugene C. Patterson was named editor. He won the Pulitzer Prize in 1967 for his daily column and editorials attacking racism and political demagoguery. Then, declaring he lacked support by his management, he left, taking control of the *St. Petersburg Times.* In the early 1980s, Thomas H. Wood headed the publishing company, Harold Gulliver was editor of the *Constitution,* and Jim Minter was executive editor. Anne Cox Chambers, daughter of the owner, became important in the company after his death. Daily circulation was 203,000.

Regional Leaders

When asked to list their regional favorites, survey respondents gave attention to a number of newspapers that did not gather enough national support to make the top fifteen list. However, their contributions have been substantial over the years and they certainly deserve the same kind of professional recognition as given more influential papers.

In the Eastern region the *Detroit Free Press* and *Detroit News* battled for circulation. Both papers were crippled by long strikes and major racial disturbances in the 1960s, and the city's unemployment problems put them deeper in financial trouble by the early 1980s. The *Free Press,* a Knight-Ridder paper, had a circulation of 635,000. David Lawrence, Jr. was the executive editor. The *News,* with Lionel Linden heading its news staff, was at 651,000. Only eight newspapers had higher circulations. Pulitzer Prizes came to both papers in the 1980s. Survey respondents in region five gave more support to the *Free Press.*

The *Baltimore Sun* continued its strong Washington coverage, but did not earn consistent national recognition. For years the paper competed strongly with the *New York Times* and *Washington Post* for a place on Washington breakfast tables, continuing a tradition for giving special attention to Washington that began with the paper's founding in 1837. The *Sun* later developed a notable foreign service and an aggressive editorial page. It is possible that the emergence of the *Philadelphia Inquirer, Boston Globe, Miami Herald, Newsday,* and other papers along the East coast cut into the *Sun's* chances to maintain its popularity with respondents. Region one voters did rank it tenth on the "top 10" list, and it finished eleventh in region eight and twelfth in region two. It had been listed in the top fifteen in 1960 and 1961 polls but dropped in subsequent surveys.

In Ohio the *Toledo Blade* gained considerable attention from the 1950s on, under the leadership of Paul Block, Jr. Giving community leadership, the *Blade* and its morning paper, the *Times,* were notable in their area. William Block owned the *Pittsburgh Post-Gazette,* another long-time leader in the region. Both papers had regional mentions.

In the Midwest the adverse climate for afternoon dailies brought mergers to Minneapolis and Des Moines. In 1961, when journalism educators listed the best combinations of morning and evening newspapers, the Cowles-owned *Minneapolis Star and Tribune* and *Des Moines Register and Tribune* were listed second and third, behind the *Louisville Courier-Journal and Times.* The *Minneapolis Star* died in 1982, with the paper becoming the morning *Star and Tribune.* In Des Moines the *Tribune* was killed, leaving the *Register* in the morning. Both surviving papers gained strong regional support and scattered national mentions, indicating the strength of their reputations.

The *Kansas City Times* got all of the attention in that area. The fabled *Kansas City Star* failed to gain much support, with the *Times* receiving strong regional recognition.

The *Chicago Sun-Times,* with its huge circulation, columnist Mike Royko, and strong editorial page, was given a flurry of regional mentions but little national recognition. Its fierce war with the *Tribune* apparently failed to spark much national attention, but the *Sun-Times* remains one of the leaders in the Midwest.

In the South, the *Charlotte Observer, Atlanta Journal, Nashville Tennessean, Memphis Commercial Appeal, Raleigh News and Observer, Richmond News Leader,* and *Arkansas Gazette* all received mentions in their regional competition.

Competition in Texas was one-sided, with the *Dallas Morning News* dominating the regional competition and the *Dallas Times Herald* coming in second. Dallas, like Chicago, has been the scene of a vigorous circulation battle, with both papers widening their coverage. Among other improvements, the *Morning News* upgraded its Washington bureau after Burl Osborne became executive editor in 1980, while Times Mirror added one hundred new staff members to the *Times Herald,* a paper purchased in 1970. Kenneth Johnson, formerly of the *Washington Post,* was executive editor of the *Times Herald.*

There were only scattered mentions of papers in the Rocky Mountain area, but in the Far West several papers demonstrated strong support, principally the *San Francisco Chronicle* and the *Seattle Times.* The *Chronicle* was favored in San Francisco over Hearst's *Examiner,* while in Seattle the *Times* held a strong lead over Hearst's *Post-Intelligencer.* The *Seattle Times* was a distant second to the *Los Angeles Times* in the Far West regional competition. The *Portland Oregonian, Sacramento Bee* and *Sacramento Union, Eugene Register-Guard,* and *San Diego Union* received scattered regional mentions.

There was immense pride felt in every quarter of the nation for the excellent work turned in by many of the smaller dailies, with a number of these papers receiving regional mentions. They are too numerous to mention, but some of their names are on the Pulitzer Prize list.